Making Potpourri Soaps & Colognes

102 Natural Recipes

David A. Webb

TAB **TAB BOOKS**
Blue Ridge Summit, PA

FIRST EDITION
SIXTH PRINTING

© 1988 by **TAB BOOKS**.
TAB BOOKS is a division of McGraw-Hill, Inc.

Library of Congress Cataloging-in-Publication Data

Webb, David A.
    Making potpourri, colognes, and soaps—102 natural recipes / by
David A. Webb.
      p.   cm.
    Includes index.
    ISBN 0-8306-9018-2   ISBN 0-8306-2918-1 (pbk.)
    1. Perfumes. 2. Potpourris (Scented floral mixtures) 3. Soap.
I. Title.
TP983.W34   1988
668'.54—dc19   88-8556
                                  CIP

TAB BOOKS offers software for sale. For information and a catalog, please contact TAB Software Department, Blue Ridge Summit, PA 17294-0850.

Questions regarding the content of this book should be addressed to:

Reader Inquiry Branch
TAB BOOKS
Blue Ridge Summit, PA 17294-0850

Edited by Suzanne L. Cheatle
Illustrated and designed by Jaclyn J. Boone

Dedicated
to Charles, Robert, Merry,
and my mother, Marion.

Contents

Acknowledgments

I WOULD LIKE TO THANK the following people and organizations for the help they provided:

Marion Michaels, Black River Falls, Wisconsin.
Dr. Robert I. Webb, Chicago, Illinois.
Mary Beth Webb, Chicago, Illinois.
Merry Michaels, Black River Falls, Wisconsin.
Charles Webb, Chippewa Falls, Wisconsin.
Mary Borofka-Webb, Chippewa Falls, Wisconsin.
Star Przybilla, Whitehall, Wisconsin.
Doris Erhardt, Black River Falls, Wisconsin.
Paul and Alvalina Nandory, Black River Falls, Wisconsin.
Hiram and Myrtle Doud, Black River Falls, Wisconsin.
David E. Clarenbach, Madison, Wisconsin.
Stephen R. Johnson, Eau Claire, Wisconsin.
Thistledown, Eau Claire, Wisconsin.
Country Treasures, Eau Claire, Wisconsin.
Elizabeth Spangler, Black River Falls, Wisconsin.
Leonard Doud, Black River Falls, Wisconsin.
Most of the photographs in this book were taken by Steve Johnson, Charles Webb, and Ziegler Studios.

Introduction

THE GIVING OF GIFTS is always in season. Think of Mom's delight when she discovers that her Mother's Day gift is potpourri made from roses from your very own garden. That aftershave cologne you've made for Dad will be sure to become his favorite. The scented soaps and sachets you make for your friends will be unique and personal gifts. You'll want to have plenty of these fragrant delights so that you have some to keep for yourself.

Making Potpourri, Colognes, and Soaps—102 Natural Recipes will help you to capture the essence of nature's most delightful aromas. With this book, you can create all your own potpourris and sachets, as well as learn to make soaps, deodorants, room fresheners, colognes, perfumes, aftershaves, and more! Also, you can do it all from natural ingredients—flowers, fruits, herbs, and spices—instead of synthetic substitutes.

This book describes in detail the particulars of blending fragrances. Certain scents complement each other; but others conflict. The novice who wishes to create his own blend should know how to harmonize fragrances.

Your garden can provide you with more than personal pleasure and leisure activity. It can produce "raw materials" you can turn into products for sale. From farmer's markets to chain stores, there's always a demand for quality home crafts.

If you don't have a garden, your grocery store might be able to provide you with many of the raw materials you'll need, so even city dwellers can participate in this craft. A comprehensive list of mail-order supply houses is included in the Appendix.

Part 1

The Basics

Chapter 1

Where to Find Ingredients

cMOST OF THE FLOWERS and fragrant herbs you will need to make potpourri and other scented products can be grown in your own garden. Many of the plants that you use will be perennials. Because they come up year after year, perennials can provide you with an annual abundance for your potpourris. Other plants are annuals, which must be sown each year. You will want to grow many of these also because they can greatly enhance your homemade goodies.

Some flowers you will select for their color and the visual properties they add to your potpourri. You will, however, choose most flowers and herbs for their fragrance. Not all attractive flowers are fragrant, and not all fragrant flowers are attractive. Because fragrance is the most important element in potpourris, it is these aromatic essences that you will want to capture.

WHICH FLOWERS TO PICK

For potpourris, you need not select your showiest blossoms. However, damaged or diseased blossoms are unacceptable. The damaged flower might rot or produce an off-scent.

Many gardeners grow some plants for show and set aside an area to grow plants for potpourris, cut flowers, and other uses. This seems to work the best for those who have the space and time to devote to gardening. Others might get their potpourri ingredients through "thinning out" some of the plants that they have.

All flowers are not equal when it comes to making potpourris and other scented products. Flowers with slight to no fragrance will not produce a scented product. Fragrant flowers are a must. Each potpourri mix should center itself around the dominant fragrance. The full details of harmonizing fragrances are discussed in the chapters that follow.

Certain flowers, such as dandelions, are added to potpourris to give color and bulk to the mix. This is especially economical if you must purchase flowers from a florist. Dandelions grow freely. They have little fragrance of their own and so will not interfere with the dominant aromas of other flowers. Of course, you must use enough of the fragrant flowers in any mix so their aroma comes through.

Chrysanthemums are also ideal for adding bulk and color to a mix. Pyrethrum petals can be added to repel insects, although this is not usually necessary since most potpourris are kept in insect-resistant containers.

Nature has its own special perfumery. Several flowers are famous for the heavenly aromas they produce. That special lingering essence of a summer's evening can be captured forever in your potpourris, colognes, candles, and soaps.

CATEGORIES OF FLOWERS

Flowers are usually divided into two or three categories, according to their life cycle. These classifications are: annuals, biennials, and perennials. Most annuals and biennials are perennials when grown in the warm climates of their origins (the tropics and subtropics). However, as many of these plants have adapted to the harsh climate of the temperate zone, they have evolved an annual life cycle; that is, they must be sown from seed each year. Annuals native to the temperate zone continue to have a perennial growth habit when raised in warm climates—at least those that adapt to such conditions.

Annuals

The seed is nature's way of procreating. Seeds are extremely hardy and can remain viable at subzero temperatures—even when the mature plant itself could not. Most annuals are abundant seed producers, which has helped them to sustain and thrive.

The annual starts from seed, planted either directly into the soil after it has warmed up and all danger of frost is past, or started in pots or *cold frames*. Cold frames are structures usually built of wood and glass to house and protect seedlings. Gardeners use them in northern climates to get an early jump on spring. The glass cover shelters plants from winds and cold temperatures, but allows the warm sunlight in. As temperatures rise, plants must be removed from the cold frame and set out into the garden so they do not get too hot. You can obtain information about cold frames from your county agricultural extension agent.

The life cycle of the annual is not very complex. It goes through its juvenile phase and forms flowers, then fruits or seeds at maturity. After flowering, the plant puts all of its energy into seed production. In most cases, it will die on or about the first frost. Seeds are dispersed by birds, wind, or small animals and insects.

Many people who save their own seeds collect the seed pods when they have "ripened" and store the seeds over winter. Hybrids will not reproduce true to seed, however. Each spring you must purchase new seeds of the desired *cultivars*, or cultivated varieties.

You can save seeds by keeping them in a place where they will be free of excess moisture, but not too dry. If there is inadequate moisture in the air, the seeds will shrivel and lose their ability to germinate. If too much moisture is present, however, seeds will rot.

You should also protect the seeds from vermin, including mice and insects. Glass jars in a cool dark room work well for storing seeds. Cover with cheesecloth or loosely fit lids to permit air circulation.

Seeds can tolerate low temperatures, but avoid placing them in areas where they might freeze. Also avoid warm areas, such as near a furnace. If seeds get too warm, they might begin to germinate.

Biennials

Biennials are very similar to annuals except for one distinction: it takes them two years to flower. For this reason, many popular biennials, such as forget-me-nots, are purchased as plants, rather than grown from seed. By purchasing nursery plants, rather than seed, you can save time and enjoy the beauty that biennials offer.

Perennials

Perennials come up year after year. With proper care, they flourish and multiply. Most perennials are among the hardiest of flowers, well-suited for people with limited time who want to establish a permanent garden.

By maintaining a perennial garden—keeping out weeds, watering and feeding plants, and dividing plants every so many years—your garden can last for a lifetime.

HERBS FOR FRAGRANCE

Several herbs are easy to grow in the home garden. The fragrant varieties will be useful to complement your flowers in potpourris. Many herbs have delightful scents of their own and can be used solely, or combined to create various aromatic bouquets.

Herbs also can be classified according to their growth habits: annuals, biennials, and perennials. When you are growing the plants in your garden, it is important to understand their growth habits.

FRAGRANCE FROM THE GROCERY STORE

Modern supermarkets sell more than just food. Most sell spices, freshly-cut flowers, herbs, and exotic and aromatic fruits, as well. People who do not have gardens, and even those who do, will find many, or most, of the items they need at the grocery store. Although some items might seem expensive, remember that only a small quantity of each ingredient is needed to make large amounts of potpourri.

Spices

It is usually not practical to grow your own cinnamon, nutmeg, or cloves. They are readily available in powdered or whole form at most groceries; for example, as cinnamon bark or clove sticks. Spices are highly aromatic and a little goes a long way. Less than an ounce of most spices will be more than enough to make plentiful batches of potpourri.

Spices are not only highly scented, they also tend to hold their fragrances for long periods of time. Rightly used, spices tend to complement and magnify floral scents. Sometimes the spices themselves produce the perfumes. Nutmeg is the dominant fragrance of a popular potpourri mix, which is especially popular around Christmas—reminiscent, perhaps, of eggnog or homemade doughnuts.

Frequently, spices are used incorrectly in a mix. Spices should be used to enhance the fragrance of the floral ingredients in a potpourri, not to mask them. Sometimes people have a heavy hand when using spices. In so doing, they actually destroy the subtle fragrances that a good potpourri reveals. In a really good potpourri, you get a mix of pleasant odors when you sniff it. It must be a harmonious mixture. It usually has a central, predominant scent, as in rose potpourri.

There are many types of spices you can use in potpourris. Some of the ones commonly employed in making potpourri include cinnamon, nutmeg, cloves, ginger, allspice, and paprika. Other spices are also useful. You probably will not want to include black pepper, as it has the tendency to make some people sneeze. For the most part, the spices you select will depend upon the illusion that you are trying to create.

A good rule of thumb
is to use spices gingerly.

Herbs

Most modern supermarkets sell herbs. Thanks in part to the back-to-nature trend, there is a consumer demand for herbs, and many stores are ready to meet that demand. If your favorite grocery store does not sell herbs, perhaps you should talk to the manager. Most stores will go out of their way to try to please their customers. A friendly conversation from you and some friends might be all it takes to get herbs on your store's shelves.

Herbs usually come in one of two forms: freshly cut, or dried. Fresh herbs might cost more and will have a much shorter shelf life than dried herbs. Dried herbs will last a long time and are ideal for making potpourris and sachets. Using dried herbs also will save you time in preparing your potpourris because herbs must be dried before they can be used in a potpourri.

Dried herbs are available in whole, cut, or powdered form. For potpourris, the cut or powdered forms are best. For sachets, the finer the grind, or powder, the better. Some people prefer to buy the whole dried herbs and grind them at home—presumably to get more of the aromatic essences of the herb. The choice is yours.

The quality of herbs depend upon how well they were stored and for how long. Most herbs will maintain their potency for several years when properly stored. Thus, whether you cut your own herbs or buy them already cut is a matter of personal preference and the amount of time you wish to spend.

The number and variety of herbs are quite large. Like spices, herbs are always expensive. If, however, you are not in position to grow your own, you will find it quite convenient to buy some. A good feature about herbs is that they can be used in minute quantities and still be effective. Unless you are making potpourris for commercial sale, the small quantities available at the grocery store usually will meet your needs.

You might want some herbs that are not so easily obtained. Rare herbs, such as deer's tongue or juniper berries usually can be purchased in health food stores or specialty shops. So can many gums and resins.

Do not overlook mail-order houses as a source of supply. The advantages of ordering by mail are many, and the chances of your getting every herb you want, including rare ones, are more secure.

Herbs can be used more freely than spices because they are not usually as pungent. Herbs also add bulk to a potpourri or sachet.

Most often, herbs are used to complement the dominant floral theme of a potpourri. Some herbs, however, have such delightful scents that they are selected to be the central theme of the potpourri. Some examples are any of the mints, especially spearmint or peppermint, and wintergreen.

Aromatic Fruits

Aromatic fruits include apples, apricots, grapes, raspberries, strawberries, and most citrus fruits, such as oranges, limes, lemons, grapefruit, and tangerines.

When fruits are used in potpourris, they are usually the central theme. Apple potpourri, for example, uses spices and herbs to accentuate the fragrance of the dried apple pieces. Often, an apple potpourri will make you think of apple pie, depending upon the spices used.

Sometimes people will blend in flower petals with a particular fruit. Rose petals seem to complement apples, grapes, raspberries, strawberries, and apricots when used in minute quantities. Orange blossoms complement most citrus potpourris. Orange potpourris are usually made from the peel, rather than the fruit of the orange. Lemongrass and other lemon-scented herbs are often combined with lemon peel for lemon potpourris.

Some fruits, such as blueberries or cherries, do not have a strong fragrance and are very difficult to capture for potpourris. Usually those fruits cannot be used because they cannot provide enough fragrance. However, often a different form of the plant can be used. For instance, the blossoms of chokecherries are extremely fragrant and will yield a heady perfume. These flowers can be used to make rare colognes and perfumes. The fruit can be dried and used in potpourris, and sachets, or as a coloring agent. Be careful not to use it to color soaps, however, because the fruit will stain your hands and clothing.

Fruits can be mixed—even apples and oranges. In fact, mixing fruits makes an interesting potpourri. Dried bananas (usually some of the peel and banana oil is used for fragrance), pineapples, coconuts, and many other fruits can be used for potpourris, sachets, scented candles, colognes, and more. It all depends upon what you want to create.

Nonfood Items

Do not forget to purchase your nonfood items at your supermarket while out shopping. Commercial lye for soapmaking is readily available and will save you time, unless you prefer to make your own lye solution from wood ashes. Lye, or caustic soda as it is sometimes called, is very concentrated and a little bit will go a long way. It should be handled very carefully. Remember when you get home to put it up in a safe place where little hands cannot possibly reach it.

Many supermarkets sell cookware. If you do not have any long-handled wooden spoons, you will want to pick up one. It will come in handy for making soap and candles. If you plan to use one for other cooking, then you had better buy two spoons. Keep the one used for soapmaking in a separate place. You would *never* use your wooden soapmaking spoon for cooking.

Chapter 2
Fabrics, Containers, and Tools

BEFORE YOU BEGIN to make potpourri, you must purchase the correct containers and tools. Your choices will be affected by your desired results. For example, if you will keep the scented products you are making, you can use less expensive materials than if you intend to sell or give away your creations. In any case, you will want to use the best tools and materials you can.

FABRICS

Although the types of cloth used for wrapping scented products might seem obvious, it usually is not. Many people do not understand the differences in cloth and other wrapping materials. These differences are important because they can determine the effectiveness of your product.

Natural vs. Synthetic

Synthetic fibers such as polyester, rayon, nylon, etc., are everywhere in modern society. They are used for virtually everything: clothing, carpeting, and wall coverings, to name a few. Each has certain characteristics that make it well suited to many purposes. For wrapping scented products, however, natural fibers, such as cotton and linen, are generally preferred.

Linen and cotton have the ability to absorb some of the fragrance into the fabric itself. Synthetics tend to be more repellent of aromatic materials, and they have tighter weaves, which do not permit as much of the fragrance through. Natural cloths breathe; synthetic cloths do not.

Made from flax, linen has been used for clothing for almost 10,000 years. Historically, it has been the choice fabric for use in sachets and other scented products. Linen absorbs large quantities of moisture, which make it ideal for handkerchiefs, towels, and napkins. It readily absorbs the fragrant oils of flowers and herbs, releasing the essence as it is flexed. Linen is very strong and durable. You can tell it from cotton by its appearance and feel. It lacks the slippery feel of many fabrics and is nubby.

Cotton is an excellent substitute for linen. The varieties of weaves and textures are virtually limitless. There are heavy cottons, like duck, and lighter variations, such as percale, gingham, and muslin. It is even possible to buy unbleached muslin for a "natural" effect.

Cotton broadcloth is cheaper than linen. Its weave is tight enough to hold most sachet powders.

Muslin is usually cheaper, but percale is more tightly woven and of better quality. It comes in an infinite array of prints or solid colors. Although linen is far superior to cotton, percale might well be the fabric you'll use for all of your needs. There is nothing more "homey" than percale.

Gingham is an excellent woven material. Most frequently, it comes in checkered form. If you use this material with fine powders, you might want to line it with cotton flour sacking, percale, or muslin, to be sure the powders do not filter through. Gingham sets a "traditional, but rustic" mood.

Burlap is good and very sturdy. It lends a rough "homespun" texture to any potpourri. At one time, it could be found free in old gunny sacks used for potatoes or animal feed. Now, however, it is recognized as a desirable material, and often can be purchased in colors. Burlap blends well with many types of contemporary furnishings. It also looks nice with colonial and oriental furnishings. However, it looks out of place in rooms designed in French provincial. In such rooms, linens or fancier cloths would be more appropriate.

You also can use fabrics of interesting texture, feel, or appearance, if desired. Corduroy and velvet come to mind. Whatever material you use, check for yourself whether it is tightly woven to hold sachet powders or meet your other uses.

Silk is acceptable, if you can afford it. One disadvantage to silk is that insects might devour it more readily than linen or cotton cloth. It will give a real luxury look for your homemade soaps and other products, however.

Linen and burlap—good fabric should breathe.

Three linens and burlap—choosing the right fabrics for your sachets is important.

You do not have to go out and buy new cloth. You can wash, dry, and cut up old flour sacks for use for sachets. Cheesecloth double layered will suffice as a wrapping for potpourris cut in large pieces or whole. The only trouble with cheesecloth even when double layered is that the wide weave might allow some of the fragmented herbs or "dust" to filter through. Cheesecloth is not as strong as some materials. Sachets, which are usually more finely ground than potpourris, might need an inner lining.

Although not as desirable as linen or cotton, it is possible to use some synthetic materials in your creations. You can choose from one of the many polyesters or nylons.

Plastic

Cheap potpourris and sachets can be made by using plastic bags. "Sandwich" or similar small bags are available at most stores. One problem with using plastic is that the bags are only moderately permeable to air. Thus, they will not permit much of the aroma of the potpourri or sachet to escape. You will need to open the bag each time you want a whiff. These bags can be time savers for those who lack the time or skill to sew linen bags and "pillows," however.

Another problem with plastic is that it looks cheap. If you are trying to sell homemade potpourris at a fleamarket or some place where people are looking for bargains, it might be acceptable. However, to use as gifts or to obtain premium prices, you will want your scented products to be wrapped in material that has much more appeal than plastic.

For sachets, plastic is impractical. Not enough scent will be released as would be if another material was used. Because the purpose of sachets is to perfume drawers, closets, and similar places, plastic wrappings defeat the purpose.

Functions of Fabric

There are many other types of cloth, or flexible materials that you can use for your potpourris and scented products. Keep in mind that the natural fibers are generally preferable to the synthetics.

The material used should perform several functions:

❀ It should be permeable enough to permit the fragrance through.
❀ It should have a tight enough weave so it will not lose the contents. Sachets usually contain fine powders, which sieve through any fabric unless the weave is very tight.
❀ Fabric should be attractive and clean. Old, dirty rags are unacceptable for holding scented products. Dirt has odors of its own, and stains detract from the beauty of the product.

Select the fabric that best suits your needs and budget. If you are skilled in sewing or embroidery, you can add fancy touches to cloth containers, if desired.

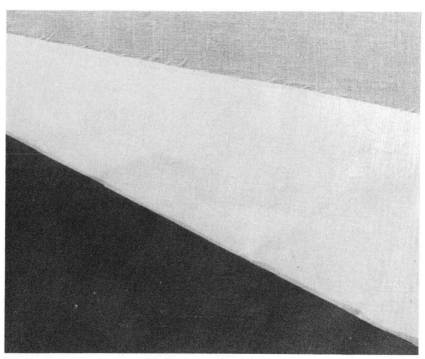

For wrapping scented products, natural fabrics are best. Cotton, poplin, and linen.

13

CONTAINERS

Much can be said about the containers you choose for your potpourris and other scented products. They should be selected with some practicality in mind. Breakable containers are all right for many homes, but people with indoor pets or small children might not want them.

You can select containers that blend with the room furnishings or that offer a sharp contrast or focal point. When choosing containers, keep in mind what you hope to achieve. The containers you choose to package your potpourris and other scented products will depend upon your preferences and budget. For marketing wares, you will want to have attractive packages.

(Stark Bros. Nurseries & Orchards Co.)

14

People are attracted by what they see. A well-dressed package gives the visual image of quality. A quality product in an ugly package will be harder to sell. In addition, a nice package can command a higher price for that very same product, which can easily translate into bigger profits for you.

Functions of Containers

A container can make an attractive display of your potpourris, but there are some things that a container cannot do. It cannot make your potpourri any better than the ingredients that you put into it. It cannot make your potpourri any more fragrant, unless the container itself has a fragrance; for example, a sandalwood bowl.

If you should be fortunate enough to have a bit of natural sandalwood to either chip into your potpourri or to use as a container, by all means do so. This wood is permeated with its own exotic oriental perfume.

Whatever you choose, there are some things that the container must do:

- ✿ A good container must be large enough to hold the potpourri without overflowing.
- ✿ The container must be leakproof (unless you enjoy sweeping up parts of your potpourri).
- ✿ The container must be sturdy. Even in the largest homes, containers are subject to occasional jarring.
- ✿ The container should not have features that tantalize the family pet, unless kept well out of reach. For example, tassels might provide a constant temptation to your cat or dog, and remember, your cat can climb.
- ✿ The container must be attractive. Ugly containers will "cheapen" the appeal of your home-scented goodies.

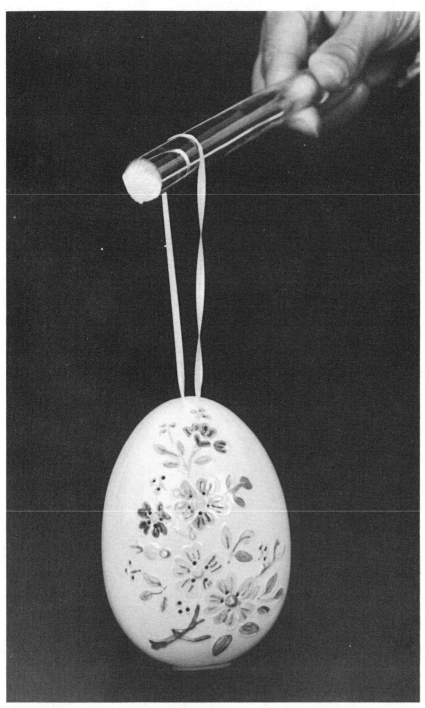

This ceramic egg can be used to hold potpourri. Note the air holes, which allow the fragrance to escape.

Types of Containers

Many types of containers can be used. Glass, ceramic, wood, and plastic containers are all available commercially. If you are talented in making ceramics, you can fashion your own dishes and ceramics.

You might already have on hand any number of attractive glass bottles or jars to exactly suit your taste. Remnants of velvet, corduroy, satin, percale, or almost any scraps of material left from your sewing might be of use. You might use last year's Christmas stockings hung briefly for decoration. Beautiful cardboard boxes can be used, or any number of items lying in your closet, house, or garage.

Your choice of material depends to some extent upon what you plan to put in your containers. For example, soap can be put into cardboard boxes, whereas perfumes would be better in glass or another waterproof vehicle.

The best way to decide what *container* to use is to first decide what your goal is. If you want to display it, you will want to make it look as glamorous as possible. If you want to sell it or give it as a present, you usually will want to package it so that it looks expensive.

Of course, if you mainly sell things at flea markets or other such places where people are definitely looking for a bargain, you need not be concerned with the package. For your own personal use, you can do without fancy containers, or use them, as you wish.

An antique tea cup would make an attractive container for potpourri in a colonial-style home.

Glass. Glass—crystal, colored, or clear—is always a good container. Open dishes will let your potpourri perfume a room. Closed containers are good for retaining the scented materials. Glass containers will store very well and allow you to see when you are getting low on your favorite colognes or perfumes.

One nice thing about glassware is that it comes in many shapes, sizes, and colors. Crystal dishes can add an air of eloquence to any potpourri, fancy soap, or candles.

Glass is a poor material for sachets, however. The aroma will not penetrate through it, unless you have a specially made glass with holes in its top. Glass fibers are not anywhere near as good as linen or cotton, and should not be used to package sachets.

Many crystal shapes add elegance and beauty to potpourris. You can use anything from a brandy snifter (for peach bloom potpourri) to a vase or a candy dish.

Ceramics. Ceramics, including porcelain, stoneware, and other clay products, is extremely popular. It can have an organic look, which lends itself to many uses. Making knickknacks or other items out of clay is a fascinating hobby, which goes hand in hand with potpourris. You might know of someone who makes their own dishes or novelty items. Nine times out of ten you will find they will be more than delighted to provide you with a sample of their wares, and perhaps sell (or possibly even give) you all you need. They also might be able and willing to fashion the packages the way you want them to look, or to offer some design ideas of their own. If you are thinking of going into business, such a friend might be willing to work for a commission, on a piecemeal basis, or on speculation.

Ceramics has many of the same qualities as glass. Both are fragile and breakable. For this reason, if you have pets or small children, you might want to consider other packaging options. Keep your homemade products in a safe place where they will not become accident victims.

Ceramic containers come in a wide range of sizes, colors, and shapes. They can be used for potpourris, soap, or candle dishes or molds, to store colognes and perfumes (provided they have a suitable cap to keep vapors inside the bottles). They are not suited for sachets, however. To get ideas for what you can do with ceramics, visit area stores that use ceramics and view their displays. Other people's designs will help you develop ideas of your own.

Wood. Do not overlook wooden dishes, containers, and boxes. Little wooden boxes shellaced with oriental motifs on them can be very attractive for displaying potpourris or storing homemade soap bars. Such boxes are readily available at many dime stores. Jewelry boxes can be converted for the purpose, and little souvenir boxes are ideal. It depends upon the size of box you are looking for.

You can sand a small souvenir box to remove the souvenir motif and restain it as you choose. Varnish stains, such as cherry, oak, maple, and others, can really make the beauty of the wood shine through. If you prefer, you can paint the little boxes. Applying coat after coat of a brightly colored (or black) enamel, Japanese style, produces a luxurious, enduring finish. You also can put on one or two coats American style. Decorative motifs for applying to wood are often available at furniture stores, or you can create your own design.

Wood is a durable container. It looks nice, while holding up well. Its advantage over ceramics and glass is that it is unbreakable. Wood can splinter, but it will not shatter into a million pieces if it falls down or is bumped by the dog or cat.

Cardboard. Cardboard boxes can be very useful for holding soap, candles, or other items. Sometimes, they are available at a delicatessen or other place that sells take-out foods. Fancy gift boxes are available at dime stores and some department stores. During the Christmas season, it's easy to find the boxes you want.

You can make cones and other special containers from paper if you are quite creative. The main drawback to using paper is that it is not very durable and is quite fragile. Unlike glass or ceramics, it tears.

(Stark Bros. Nurseries & Orchards Co.)

20

You can display your potpourris in various ways.
People judge products by the way they are packaged.

Other Materials. Your imagination is your only limitation to what you can use to package potpourris and your other scented products. Rubber, burlap, grass, and woven straw are a few of the items you can use. Remember that whatever you use should be durable, attractive, and able to store the product without adding undesirable odors. If it is a closed container, it should allow the fragrance of the product to come through (except for perfume, of course).

Cover or Not

Another aspect of containers that you will want to consider is whether to use open containers, such as dishes, or containers that are covered. The type of container you use for potpourris is mostly a matter of choice. Sachets, naturally have to be enclosed since they are often placed in direct contact with clothes. Perfumes and colognes would evaporate rapidly if left uncovered in their bottles.

Sometimes, people like to use dishes that have covers with air holes in them. One advantage to these covers is that they allow the smell to filter through, while still providing the practicality of a cover. If the dish is tipped over, only a small amount of the contents spills out. With an open dish, you can lose the entire contents if the dish tips over.

Fabric covers are perhaps most popular, for several reasons. First, they allow the aroma to penetrate and perfume the surroundings. Second, they are unbreakable. Although fabric is subject to tearing, it usually will not come apart unless the cat has been playing with it (or the dog or kids).

Large covered jars can be used to store potpourri. When you use the potpourri, use containers with slits in the tops to allow the fragrance to escape into the room. Ceramic dishes are used to display scented soaps. Metal boxes are pleasing to the eye. (Thistledown)

Color

Some people prefer colorful containers; others like those that are more subdued. Bright colors are especially attractive and add to the excitement of sachets and potpourris, whether they are given or sold. A splash of color can enliven any room. Pastel tones add their own charm to your creations, whether they take the form of a muted rainbow or one solid tint.

If you feel it unsophisticated to use colors that make your potpourris stand out, disguise them by selecting materials that blend with the fabrics used in your rooms. You can place potpourris in discreet locations where they will not be obvious, if you prefer.

TOOLS

The only way to make anything right is to use the right tools. If you use equipment that is ill suited to the purpose, you will not achieve a quality product. Do not shortchange yourself. Take the time to do the job right. Line up all the tools you will need to complete each task.

New tools are not essential, providing that the old equipment is still in good condition. If the equipment you use is not in top shape, you could ruin the product or injure yourself.

The best way to have the tools you need when you want them is to take care of them. After each use, wash, dry, and store them in a special drawer, box, or area where you will be able to find them again. Keep tools in a place where young children will not have access to them. Children love to play with things and scatter them all around. If your tools are not put up out of reach, you might never find some of them again.

Use tools properly. Do not use a spoon handle, screwdriver, or putty knife for prying open jars. Don't use barber shears to cut paper, nor light cloth shears to cut denim. Everytime you misuse your tools, you shorten their life span. Spoons that are broken or bent are not as handy as those that are straight. Pans without handles are dangerous when removed from or put on hot stoves. If you use your tools only for the purpose for which they are intended, you will spare yourself much grief.

Types of Tools

Most tools needed to make potpourris and other scented products are readily available at the dime store, drugstore, or supermarket. Many tools you will find in your cupboards. Some specialized tools you might wish to buy.

Mortar and Pestle. If you grow many of your own herbs and a few of your spices, you might want to possess a mortar and pestle. A *mortar* is a small marble bowl that is polished except for the inside base. The *pestle* is a marble stick, polished except for its end. These nonpolished areas are used for grinding the herbs and spices.

Marble mortar and pestle sets are commerically available at a moderate price. They might also be a good investment if you wish to grind your own spices and herbs. Some people believe that the way to get the most fragrance from spices and herbs is by grinding them fresh. Others are content with purchasing spices and herbs in their powdered (already-ground) form.

Tea Infusers and Tea Balls. To use many herbs, you might want to first make them into a "tea" or liquid. To do so, you will need something to separate the solid matter from the fluid. It is important to remove the solid matter (dredges) in making products such as homemade soaps and candles, where the appearance of the finished product is important. In the case of soaps, you will not want any solids that leave a "grainy feel" in the soap because they likely will irritate tender skin.

Tea infusers and tea balls come in many forms. Tea balls usually have a little chain for dipping them into and out of the water. They hold cut herbs so that they are not lost into the tea itself. By keeping the two separate, you can control the strength of your solution.

Tea balls and infusers come in many colors and are made in different materials, including steel, porcelain, and plastic. Steel and porcelain types are perhaps more useful than the plastic. Although the plastic types are cheaper, they have been known to melt or crack if water used in the preparation of the solution was too hot, or if they were inadvertently set too close to an open flame or burner.

Scale. A scale to measure the weights of dry or liquid ingredients might be useful if you plan to produce products for sale, or on a large basis. Ordinary kitchen scales can measure ingredients accurately and conveniently. They are most useful when recipes are given on a per-weight basis. Usually, you will find that an ordinary measuring cup can give a good estimate of dry ingredients. If you are a stickler for detail, however, or have an old recipe book that measures items according to weight or parts, a scale might be a handy investment.

Eyedropper. There will be times when you need only a drop or two of some precious floral or herbal oil. Such oils are extremely potent. To measure out oil for perfume, an eyedropper is a handy tool.

One advantage of an eyedropper is that it allows you to measure, in precise and minute quantities, liquid ingredients. Without this tool, you might be apt to waste or spill precious oils, or put too much or too little of fragrant oils into your recipes.

Other Tools. For making soap and candles, a large kettle is ideal. Buy one, or use one already on hand. Once you use a pan for soapmaking, however, never use it for cooking foods again.

The kettle should have secure handles so that it will be easy to carry it from the heat source to a place to cool off. A kettle without handles or an old kettle with wobbly handles might slip and spill hot soap or hot wax. Soap burns get much hotter than water, and they stick to your skin and continue burning. It is wiser and more economical in the long run to simply buy a good kettle with handles, rather than to use an old one with a loose screw or some parts missing.

A large wooden spoon is very useful in making soaps and/or preparing other items. Wood is a preferred utensil because it will not conduct heat as rapidly as metal, thus lessening the chance of burns.

A large wooden spoon also will be useful for stirring potpourris and sachets. Large spoons carry more leverage with them, so you do not have to work as hard to mix ingredients as you do when using a smaller spoon. You also can use your wooden spoon somewhat as a pestle to grind up herbs and spices.

A measuring cup and set of measuring spoons are absolute musts for your tool collection. You cannot follow any recipe if you do not measure ingredients as accurately as possible. It is much easier for you to follow recipes and even create recipes of your own when you are using proper measuring tools.

Jars with tight lids are very important when you are dealing with fragile and volatile aromas, such as floral oils. Often in mixing ingredients you will want to trap vapors to seal the fragrance into the mixture. To succeed, you will need bottles with tight-fit caps. When using Mason jars, you should wrap tape around the top to seal all exposed areas.

Clean Tools

It is always a good idea to take care of your tools. That way, you will not have to replace them as often. If you clean tools as soon as possible after each use, they will be ready when you need them again.

The chore of cleaning tools is lessened when they are cleaned right away. Most items clean best when the foul matter is still fresh. If allowed to set, they can become more difficult to clean. When cleaning tools, be careful to not break them. Broken tools can be dangerous to work with.

Frequently, it is not possible to clean tools immediately after you use them. When it is not, let them set until you have finished your entire operation. Then, begin cleaning the tools right away.

Be sure that your tools are thoroughly dried before you put them into storage. Most metals tend to form rust. Spots of water left on them accelerates the rust. Dry off each tool then set it away. Some tools need to be oiled. You should oil anything especially prone to rust after each use. If the instrument is used for heating, however, it is important to remove the oil before using it by wiping the tool dry with paper toweling, and probably rinsing it on the outside with warm water.

Part 2

Specific Ingredients & Special Recipes

Chapter 3

Floral and Other Scents

IF YOU ARE not an avid gardener you might ponder the advantages of growing your own flowers for perfumes, colognes, and sachets. One reason is economy. Floral oils are often costly, although usually only a few drops are needed. Even if you live in a city apartment or do not own any land, you can still grow flowers indoors in pots. Another consideration is that flowers add so much to the beauty of a home.

You will discover that there is a special thrill in growing your own flowers and using them to produce fragrant delights. For this purpose, you should always plant the most fragrant species and varieties. Pick garden flowers so that they are whole. Keep the varieties separate by placing a layer of cloth between each bunch. Place flowers in a basket or sack. Be careful to not crush them.

If you lack a certain desired flower or your garden crop did not yield as expected, do not despair. You can buy almost any kind of flowers from the florist. One or two are probably all you will need, unless you are making a large batch or bulk-marketing products. You might even be able to get a few blossoms from a friend, especially if that person might later be a recipient of one of your special creations.

If you lack the time or patience to grow your own flowers and herbs, remember that floral oils and herbs are available from specialized shops and mail-order houses. (See Appendix.)

GARDEN FLOWERS AND SHRUBS

Most flowers are easy to grow. Annuals are best grown from seed because plants are very expensive and live for only one season. If you are pressed for time, you might not wish to plant annuals because of the amount of labor required and the need to replant them every year. After they have blossomed, however, most people concede that they are worthwhile.

Biennials and perennials can be started from seed, but are more easily set out as young plants. The plants are worth the extra cost because they can save a year's growing time. They also allow you to space the garden, eliminating the chore of thinning out unwanted plants as is needed when plants are started with seed. Biennials have a two-year life span, although in warmer climates they may reseed themselves. The biennial grows the first summer and blooms the next.

Perennial plants usually bloom the first year set out, so there is no long wait. You can plant your garden in the spring after the ground can be worked and enjoy blossoms the very same summer.

Fragrant Annuals

Some of the best annuals for fragrance are the following.

Sweet alyssum, *Lobularia maritima*, produces very fragrant flowers on compact plants. There are many excellent varieties available in a wide range of colors—from white to rose-pink and violet.

Sweet pea, *Lathyrus odoratus*, comes in a wide range of colors. There are compact plants, as well as "climbers." All are enjoyably fragrant.

Flowering tobacco,—*Nicotiana alata* or *Nicotiana x hybrida* are two of the best selections—is available in different sizes, from dwarfs to larger varieties. Flowering tobacco produces flowers with a noticeable and agreeable aroma.

Snapdragons, *Antirrhinum majus*, was probably one of the favorite flowers in your grandmother's garden. It is still popular, and for good reasons: snapdragons provide both beauty and fragrance to the family garden.

Virginia stock, *Malcolmia maritima*, is also a flower that was once grown more widely than today. It is available in separate or mixed colors, and is very fragrant.

Carnations, *Dianthus caryophyllus*, produce a spicy clovelike scent. Although perennial species are available, most are only moderately hardy in the northern states, and they lack the size of blossoms that the annuals bear. One of the best cultivars is Giant Chaubaud. Perennial species and "pinks" can be used by those who prefer an all perennial garden.

The perennial sweet pea is a flower noted for its delightful fragrance. Shown is the Bijou Mixed Sweet Pea. (Burpee)

Fragrant Biennials

Sweet william, *Dianthus barbatus*, is a distant cousin to the carnation, but is much hardier. They are low-growing plants. Sweet williams are characterized by their catlike markings.

Fragrant Perennials

A perennial garden is a joy that, with simple care and maintenance, can last a lifetime. Perennials are a favorite of people for their ease of growing and for the beauty and fragrance they bring each year as they bloom. Some of the best perennials follow.

Roses are a favorite of most people. There are three species that are especially noted for their fragrance: *Rosa rugosa*, *Rosa damascena*, and *Rosa x hybrida*.

The rugosa shrub roses are extremely hardy and can be grown throughout most of the United States and much of Canada. They produce fragrant and showy flowers and large rose hips, which are also used in potpourris, teas, and other items. Some of the best rugosa selections are: Magnifica, Sir Thomas Lipton, and Alba.

Damask roses are the ones from which rose attar is obtained. These floral oils are very expensive and require a great number of blossoms. A damask rose that is readily available in the United States is Madame Hardy; other selections also can be found at some nurseries.

Hybrid tea roses are the most popular. These are the long-stemmed florist's roses. Most are not as fragrant as other roses. There are, however, many selections that are fragrant: Lincoln, Fragrant Cloud, Crimson Glory, Mirandy, John F. Kennedy, Proud Land, and so many more. Check with your nursery to see what varieties are available.

The aforementioned roses do not entail a listing of all of the fragrant rose species and cultivars in the world. Only those that are readily available at most nurseries are given. When purchasing hybrid tea roses, keep in mind that they are not winter hardy in the far north. If you are fortunate to have wild roses in your yard, you will not wish to overlook them as a good perfume source.

The peony, *Paeonia x hybrida*, is often overlooked. When in bloom it is one of the showiest flowers in the garden, and very fragrant as well. The size of blooms and their tantalizing fragrance make them ideal for potpourris. Two excellent cultivars are Edulis superba, and Karl Rosenfeld.

Lilacs from your garden can be used to scent soaps and sachets.

Lilacs, *Syringa* sp., have all the romance of an April vacation in Paris. As easy-to-grow shrub with beautiful and intensely fragrant flowers, they are almost a must for anyone with growing space. Several species, as well as hybrids, are available. Fragrant cultivars include Dwarf Korean, Japanese Tree, Persian, and any of the French hybrids.

The primrose, *Primula vulgaris*, is a fragrant way to line a garden path. It comes in many colors.

The Missouri primrose, *Oenthera missouriensis*, is not a true primrose. When open in the late afternoons and evenings, its flowers give off a delightful scent. It produces hardy yellow flowers.

True geraniums, *Pelargonium* sp., come in many fragrant varieties and grow easily. Geraniums are fine for potpourris, or to scent perfumes, candles, and soaps.

Unscented Flowers

Flowers that lack a strong or definable aroma are excellent additions to potpourris. Dandelions are an example. They grow like weeds and can add bulk and color to any potpourri, despite their very slight fragrance.

For other potpourris, you might prefer to use petunia blossoms. Petunias bloom all summer long and come in a wide splash of colors. They can add floral petals to your mix, and they are almost always cheaper than florist's flowers.

Chrysanthemums are another excellent flower. Their faint odor does not interfere with dominant fragrances. An ideal feature of this flower is the amount of bulk it can give to a potpourri. One football mum blossom can provide enough material for several potpourris.

"Mums" are easy flowers to grow and are hardy almost everywhere. They come in pompon and other sizes, both of blossoms and of plants. Dwarf plants are handy for those with small yards or limited space. They are also nice for growing in containers. Only a few mums will produce plenty of material for your potpourris.

WOODLAND SCENTS

There is nothing as exhilarating as a walk in the forest. The fresh, clean fragrances tickle your senses. The aromas in nature are, of course, a natural potpourri of the different flowers, leaves, bark, and plants that grow in the wild. You can duplicate this effect in your woodland garden.

Most flowers grow best along the forest's edge where they can get some sunshine, or in open spaces in the woods. Some flowers, however, prefer slightly shaded conditions and bloom well in areas where they receive only indirect sunlight.

Lily of the valley, *Convallaria majalis*, is a favorite old-fashioned fragrance for perfumes. It can also be used in sachets, soaps, candles, and colognes. These tiny flowers command attention because of the powerful, intoxicating fragrance that they pack.

Alkanet, *Anchusa capensis*, is an annual that grows about 1½ feet tall. It has very fragrant petals that resemble forget-me-nots. There is also a perennial species, *Anchusa azurea*, which grows up to 5 feet tall.

Mignonette, *Reseda odorata*, grows to about 1½ feet. It has an attractive display of red flowers with a delightful fragrance. Sow in a sunny location. Add lime to the soil before sowing seed for best growth.

Violets

English violets, *Viola odorata* are a favorite of the scented woodland flowers. They are also the choice of fine florists. These long-stemmed fragrant beauties can be picked for small bouquets. They are excellent for potpourris and make especially elegant sachets. You will want to grow plenty of them, since they are ideal for perfumes, colognes, and soap.

VIOLET POTPOURRI
1 quart violet blossoms
2 tablespoons salt
½ ounce powdered orris root (its fragrance resembles violets.)
1 ounce powdered benzoin gum
1 cup of rose petals or 1/16 ounce rose oil
2 ounces of deodorized cognac

Crush violet petals tightly into a quart Mason jar. Add the remaining ingredients. Stir well and store with a tight lid. If you use fresh blossoms, the mixture will take a few weeks to settle. If you use dried flowers, your potpourri will be ready as soon as the ingredients have been thoroughly mixed.

To enhance the violet fragrance, add a drop of your homemade violet perfume to the mix. Sachets, especially, should be given extra potency.

Witch Hazel

The bark of witch hazel, *Hamamelis virginiana*, once distilled, makes a fragrant solution used in aftershaves and astringents. You can use powdered bark in potpourris, but make it into a tincture first when you are using it in sachets to release the true potency of the fragrance. You can make a tincture of witch hazel as follows.

Grind 1 ounce powdered witch hazel bark to a fine powder with your mortar and pestle. Add 6 ounces of unscented alcohol.

You can add the tincture to the dry ingredients. If used in a potpourri, add a drop or two of the tincture as the last ingredient before the lid is closed. Mix it in well with the dry ingredients.

Do not drown a potpourri or sachet. If the mix gets too wet, it will not function, being too messy as a sachet for drawers. If the mix forms clumps, let it set. After a few days when it has dried, break up the clumps.

Balsam

Balsam fir, *Abies balsamea*, produces needles that are delightfully fragrant when dried. They are used in sachets, added to bath salts, soaps, and candles. The balsam makes a better Christmas tree than the spruce, both because of this fragrance and because its leaves remain longer on the tree.

Resins from the balsam fir are also useful. They make an excellent glue. If dried, they can be ground up into a powder for use in sachets, both to add fragrance and to help retain other fragrant volatile oils.

Forget-Me-Nots

Forget-me-nots, *Myosotis alpestris*, are biennials with a more or less perennial growth habit. The named forms will come true from seed. Small growing, they are a must for any fragrant garden.

Because forget-me-nots are very small flowers, it takes quite a few blossoms to produce a good sachet, and more are needed for making perfume. They are usually made into a tincture to capture their fragrance. The tincture is then added to sachets or perfumes to provide the fragrance. Because a great deal of bulk is needed in potpourris, you can add chrysanthemum blossoms to provide the extra bulk.

FORGET-ME-NOT POTPOURRI
1 quart dried chrysanthemum blossoms
1 pint dried 'Heavenly Blue' morning glory petals
½ ounce powdered benzoin gum
2 tablespoons salt
3 drops tincture of forget-me-nots

Prepare tincture of forget-me-nots by adding 1 ounce of forget-me-nots to 6 ounces of unscented alcohol. Cover the mixture and let it sit overnight, shaking the contents occassionally. Strain the solids off after the alcohol has dissolved the volatile fragrant oils of forget-me-nots. Keep the liquid tincture covered with a tight lid to prevent loss to evaporation.

When making any tincture, use the strongest potency alcohol available. If available, 90 percent by volume is the best because it gives off the strongest aromas.

After the potpourri is ready, you can place it into other containers. Put another drop of tincture of forget-me-nots in each jar if you desire a stronger fragrance.

Note: Directions for making potpourri are given in Chapter 6. You can add other herbs and spices to any of these recipes, as desired. Any good potpourri is a harmony of aromas with one dominant theme.

PLANTS GATHERED FROM THE WILD

Although many flowers grow in the wild, it might not be practical to gather them. Also, it might be illegal. Some wildflowers are protected by law. It is best to check with the authorities before picking any wildflowers.

Most of these flowers can easily be grown at home. Seed companies offer a tremendous display of improved varieties. The cost for seed is fairly economical. Some nurseries even offer young transplants, which are especially practical for those who have difficulty trying to get anything to grow from seed, and for those who do not like to wait too long before they can see some concrete results.

Not all of the scents of the woods are flowers, of course. Trees, bushes, grasses, and other forms of life all add to the aromas. Unpleasant odors you will not want to imitate.

Usually the leaves, fruits, flowers, bark, or roots of a tree or shrub are the parts that are most aromatic. It depends upon the plant as to which feature is its most fragrant asset. In the case of maples, however, the sap is more aromatic.

Maple Sugar

Maple sap gives a more realistic smell of maple than do the leaves, which rapidly decompose. One problem with maple sap is that it will turn rancid if left to itself, so maple sugar is the best choice to capture the essence of the maple. The sugar, although usually expensive, can be purchased through mail-order outlets. If you live in "maple country" you can probably buy some directly from a grower. Being sugar it is a natural preservative. A can of maple sugar will go far, since only a small amount is needed for potpourris and sachets.

An economical way to get maple sugar is to mix maple syrup with white granulated sugar. The sugar will prevent the syrup from turning rancid.

MAPLE SUGAR
1 cup white granulated sugar
3 tablespoons real maple syrup

Stir the mix until it is uniform in color. If it is still moist, let it dry off in an oven for a minute or two. Do not bake it, however. If you added too much syrup, simply add more white sugar to get to the right consistency.

Pine

Almost all pines are aromatic. The needles are especially fragrant when bent or flexed. Any of the pines in your area will probably do nicely. Do not strip a tree of all of its needles. Only a handful or two are needed for most purposes. Use only green needles. Brown-colored (usually fallen) needles will have a lesser and different scent than green needles. Green needles are much more aromatic.

If you are gathering needles from more than one type of pine, you might wish to separate the bunches from each tree. Doing so will give you an opportunity to compare your formulas for which is the most fragrant. It also will allow you to duplicate your recipes to exact measures.

The white pine, *Pinus strobus*, and the Scotch pine, *Pinus sylvestris*, are two pine species with fragrant needles.

Cedar

You can purchase cedar chips to scent closets as well as keep out moths and other obnoxious insects. The smell of cedarwood repels many insects, but is very pleasing to most people. It is recommended that no wood-type potpourri be prepared without at least a few cedar chips mixed in.

Cedar panels are usually expensive at lumberyards. By making your own potpourri from cedar chips, you can achieve the same effects of mothproofing your closets and wardrobes at a fraction of the cost. To keep potpourris potent, you might want to add a drop or two of cedarwood oil every year.

Cedar chips will deodorize your home and keep moths out of your closets.

Sandalwood

Sandalwood gives off a rich, oriental aroma. It is one of the most fragrant natural woods. It also has the quality of being a fixative agent, in that it can capture and release scents. It is a must for incense.

Because sandalwood is native to India, you might need to purchase it in the form of wood, chips, or oil.

WOODLAND POTPOURRI
8 ounces of balsam fir needles
4 ounces of pine needles
3 ounces of maple sugar
2 ounces cedarwood chips or one drop cedarwood oil
3 ounces of sandalwood chips, or one drop of sandalwood oil
   (if available)
1 ounce sweet woodruff.

If you do not include sandalwood chips (or oil) in this recipe, then add 1 ounce of powdered benzoin gum, or powdered balsam Peru.

Use your imagination to create woodland scents of your own making. Just remember to balance the fragrances so that the stronger scents do not overshadow the weaker.

MEADOW SCENTS

The fresh smell of a summer meadow is hard to match. You can capture some of the delightful essences by adding fragrant grasses and herbs to your potpourris, sachets, and other scented products.

Sweet woodruff, *Asperula odorata*, is a low-growing species that is useful as a ground cover. Most remarkable about this plant is that its leaves, when crushed, smell like newly mown hay. Because of this delightful characteristic, it is especially sought after for sachets. It really captures the essence of a summer meadow and those warm summer grasses.

To use the leaves of sweet woodruff, dry them as you would flowers and place them into your sachets. You can capture their essence for perfumes by making a tincture first. To prepare a tincture, mix 1 ounce of sweet woodruff leaves to 6 ounces of alcohol. Let the mixture sit overnight in a tightly covered jar. Strain off solids when the liquid is heavily perfumed.

OLD ENGLISH POTPOURRI
1 quart English lavender petals
½ pint rosemary
1 pint rose petals
½ ounce powdered orris root
1 ounce powdered frankincense
¼ ounce powdered myrrh
2 tablespoons salt
1½ teaspoons of cinnamon

By using dried flowers and leaves, you can use the mix after it has been stirred up.

English lavender, *Lavandula spica*, is one of the oldest flowers used in sachets. It has set the standard for so many generations that lavender is frequently thought of as *the* flower for sachets.

Lavender is highly fragrant. Kept in a sealed container, its fragrance can remain potent for several years. Lavender is so strongly fragrant that it tends to impart some of its fragrance on anything it touches. This is one reason why lavender is a favorite sachet. Stuck in a drawer with undergarments or socks, it will leave them smelling flowery fresh.

Lavender is also great for scenting soaps. It can be used in colognes and perfumes, as well. If you grow no other flower, grow lavender.

Lavender

Heather

Scottish heather, *Calluna vulgaris*, is another old-time favorite. It is sometimes used in conjunction with lavender; sometimes by itself. Lavender tends to be the dominant fragrance when the two are combined in equal parts so, to emphasize the heather, you will want to use only a touch of lavender in your recipe.

The lovely smell of Scottish heather will have you reaching for a kilt and bagpipe. It is easy to grow and grows well in poor soils where other plants might not flourish. Gather the flowers to dry them for sachets.

SCOTTISH HEATHER POTPOURRI
1 pint dried heather blossoms
1 cup dried sweet woodruff
¼ cup (four ounces) dried lavender petals
½ ounce powdered orris root
1 ounce powdered benzoin gum

Mix ingredients well. If you use fresh flowers, you will need to dry the mixture.

Note: You may always add any of your favorite herbs, dried flowers, and spices to any potpourri or sachet. To keep the fragrances in balance, however, it is best to not use flowers or spices that will overshadow your favored fragrances.

Bee balm, *Monarda didyma*, does attract bees to its colorful blossoms. The bees can make wax for your homemade candles, as well as honey for your palate.

Bee balm has a pleasant "citrusy" aroma and is easy to grow. Another common name for bee balm is bergamot. Oil of bergamot is used to flavor tea, as well as to scent perfumes. The wild bergamot, *Monarda fistulosa*, is one of the most pungent species.

Lemongrass

Lemon is a favorite smell. Many commercial products are given a lemon aroma to broaden their appeal in the marketplace. You might find it desirable to create your own lemon-scented products.

Lemongrass, *Thymus* x *citriodorus*, is sometimes called *lemon thyme*. It can become confusing since there are many different species called lemongrass.

This species grows to only about 4 inches in height. It is a dwarf, compact plant that will fit in any yard. It has small, delicate leaves that smell like lemons. The aroma of lemons is strongest when the leaves are crushed.

Lemongrass is an excellent plant for sachets and other scented products where a hint of lemon is desired. It can be used as a substitute for lemon, or in combination with dried lemon peel. In the making of soaps, eau de colognes, and perfumes, combine tincture of lemongrass with the oil.

LEMON-SCENTED ROOM FRESHENER
1 pint unscented alcohol
3 ounces tincture of lemongrass
2 ounces tincture of lemon peel
1 ounce sweet woodruff (tincture)
½ cup liquid chlorophyll
1 ounce tincture of balsam Peru

Mix ingredients well. Pour the liquid into an atomizer. Store the excess liquid in a tightly covered jar. If you do not have an atomizer, any of the "plant misters" sold in most dime stores make an excellent substitute. Be sure to use *tinctures* of gums, resins, and other aromatic materials to keep from clogging the spray nozzles.

Newly Mown Potpourri

If you are among the people who love the smell of a newly mown lawn, take heart. That delightful aroma, too, can be captured. To do so, you must make a tincture of your grass clippings. For the best fragrance, add a small amount of sweet woodruff.

You can make a tincture of grass by adding 1 cup (8 ounces) of grass clippings to 1 pint of unscented alcohol. Let the ingredients sit overnight so that the volatile oils can dissolve into the alcohol. Be certain that the jar has a tight lid so that vapors cannot escape. After most of the chlorophyll and fragrant oils have dissolved into the alcohol solution, it is ready for use. Strain off the solid matter (or dregs).

NEWLY MOWN POTPOURRI
1 ounce sweet woodruff
½ ounce orris root powder
3 ounces dried alfalfa
1 ounce dried rose petals
3 drops of tincture of grass
2 tablespoons salt

WILDFLOWERS

One of the delights of a meadow are the wildflowers that grow there. Such flowers as the butterfly weed, coreopsis, black-eyed Susan, asters, flax, lupines, poppies, and more tickle the imagination.

Many of these wildflowers are best noted for their looks and not their aromas. Some are more fragrant than others. While not all are suited to perfumery, they all have some scent that can add to the charm of your scented products.

Wildflowers differ in various areas of the country. You can prepare a potpourri from those native to your area, or elsewhere. If you wish to collect wildflowers from the countryside, you will probably prepare your potpourris from the flowers that grow near you. If you grow wildflowers in your garden, you will have a greater selection.

Remember that some wildflowers are protected by law. Some are not to be picked even on your own land. Before you gather any wildflowers, first check with your county agricultural agent.

Also, do not assume that because you are out in the country everything is free. Most land is owned by individuals or families. Just as you would object to someone coming into your yard and picking your flowers, so do many country landowners object to intruders. Always check with the owner first. It could save you from a court appearance on trespass charges later.

Most of the flowers that you will want to pick will be obvious, but do not pick them all. Leave some wildflowers to grow and beautify the area, and provide future seed. If you pick them all, no new flowers will spring up after the old die out. Be a good steward of nature. Others will appreciate the opportunity to enjoy the wildflowers' beauty.

To best preserve the whole blossoms, pick flowers at the stem level. Carry along a basket or paper bag to place flowers into once picked. Something that will not crush the petals works best. If you wish to dry the flowers afterwards, you will want them to be in recognizable form. Even if the flowers will later be made into sachets or potpourris, you will not want them crumbled and mangled. The flowers will make better potpourris if they are dried before they are torn apart. This method helps to maintain the integrity of floral oils as well.

Keep different flowers separate by placing a layer of paper toweling between the bunches. It is easier to do it this way than to carry separate containers for each species of flower that you pick. One reason to keep bunches separate is to give yourself a clear idea of what flowers you are using in your mix. Also it is easier to measure the flowers for uniform batches when they are kept separate.

If you wish to grow your own wildflowers, you can obtain wildflower seeds in many nurseries. (See Appendix.)

Chapter 4

Southern Flowers, Fruits, Spices, and Herbs

THE WARM, SUBLIME climate of most southern states lends itself to a wide selection of fragrant flowers. Robust jasmine, tantalizing honeysuckle, heady gardenias, and that favorite for many traditional weddings, the citrusy orange blossoms, all come to mind.

SOUTHERN FLOWERS

Jasmine, *Jasminum polyanthum*, produces a fragrance that complements the essences of other flowers in perfumes.

Some flowers and flowering shrubs are unique to the South. Gardenia, *Gardenia jasminoides*, is a shrub with waxy leaves. It is as ornamental as it is fragrant, producing pure white blossoms that just reek of perfume. Gardenias, with their heady aroma, are a must for any southern garden.

There are many types of honeysuckles to choose from. An everblooming species is *Lonicera* x *heckrotti*.

Hall's honeysuckle, *Lonicera japonica* or halliana, is ever popular. For compact growth, you might wish to choose the *Lonicera periclymenum*; one of their best cultivars is Serotina Florida.

The camellia, *Camellia japonica*, is one of the most fragrant members of the camellia family. It can be grown in a greenhouse up North. Its beauty is unmatched when in full bloom.

The Japanese wisteria, *Wisteria floribunda*, is slightly more hardy than the Chinese wisteria, *Wisteria sinensis*. Both are fragrant species, most famous for their grapelike clusters of flowers when in blossom.

Heliotrope
Marine

Heliotrope, *Heliotropium peruvianum*, is an annual best grown indoors as a potted plant. It can be grown in the South, but must be taken inside whenever temperatures dip below 45°F. Heliotrope produces one of the most intoxicating perfumes.

Freesias, *Freesia refracta*, are a florist's favorite. They have a robust fragrance and do well in all but the deep South.

You can obtain many of these flowers from friends and relatives, or from your florist.

Recipes

The following are some excellent recipes that will remind you of a stroll in a southern garden. You can also make up your own mixtures.

HELIOTROPE POTPOURRI
1 pint dried heliotrope blossoms
2 tablespoons salt
1 ounce powdered benzoin gum
½ cup (4 ounces) dried rose petals
2 teaspoons vanilla extract
1 cup (8 ounces) dried petunia blossoms

JASMINE POTPOURRI
1 pint dried jasmine petals
½ pint dried rose petals
1 tablespoon brown sugar
2 tablespoons salt
½ ounce powdered orris root

GARDENIA POTPOURRI
1 pint dried gardenia blossoms
½ pint dried rose petals
½ pint dried jasmine petals
1 ounce powdered balsam Peru
2 tablespoons salt

NEW ORLEAN POTPOURRI
4 ounces dried rose petals
8 ounces dried jasmine blossoms
2 ounces dried gardenia flowers
2 ounces dried bee balm blossoms or 1 drop oil of bergamot
½ ounce dried lavender flowers

CAMELLIA POTPOURRI
8 ounces dried camellia blossoms
4 ounces dried petunia blossoms
½ ounce powdered orris root
4 ounces dried rose petals
2 tablespoons salt

HONEYSUCKLE POTPOURRI
8 ounces dried honeysuckle blossoms
4 ounces dried rose petals
2 ounces dried gardenias
1 drop oil of bergamot
1 ounce powdered balsam Tolu

DALLAS POTPOURRI
8 ounces dried yellow rose petals
4 ounces dried red rose petals
2 ounces dried jasmine
2 ounces dried heliotrope blossoms
1 teaspoon cloves
2 ounces dried gardenia petals
2 tablespoons salt
1 ounce powdered balsam Tolu

MIAMI POTPOURRI
8 ounces orange blossoms
1 ounce shredded orange peel
1 ounce shredded tangerine peel
½ ounce shredded lemon peel
2 ounces dried gardenia petals
½ ounce jasmine flowers
4 ounces bee balm blossoms or 2 drops oil of bergamot
1 ounce balsam Peru

WISTERIA POTPOURRI
8 ounces dried wisteria blooms
4 ounces dried rose petals
2 ounces dried violets
2 ounces dried lilac blooms
1 ounce dried jasmine petals
½ ounce orris root powder
2 tablespoons salt

Designs

The containers you select for your products can reflect the mood created by the aroma itself. Different designs may be desired on your packages; for example, a picture of a riverboat or plantation that brings back the era of the Antebellum South.

Avoid negative images, however. Any design that refers to slavery is likely to be offensive to the world at large and many of your friends.

The South offers a wider display of horticultural material to choose from than most other regions of the United States. This does not mean, however, that you can't add flowers from other regions. For example, the addition of lilacs or other northern blossoms will enhance most floral mixes.

If you do not grow your own flowers, you can purchase them in the quantity that you desire from a local farmer, grower, or even a relative. You do not have to pay florist's prices for many flowers. They do not need to be florist perfect to be used in sachets or other items.

Old flowers are not as fragrant as freshly cut ones. In addition, it will take fewer freshly cut blossoms to produce your homemade bouquets than it will using fading, dying blossoms.

FRUITS AND SPICES

Aromatic fruits can be divided into three categories:

- ❀ Temperate zone fruits
- ❀ Citrus fruits
- ❀ Other tropical and subtropical fruits

Most people in the United States will be able to grow temperate-zone fruits. Those lucky enough to live in California, Hawaii, Florida, Texas, and similar climes will be able to grow citrus and, with some care, other tropical and subtropical fruits.

Temperate-Zone Fruits

Apples, *Malus pumila.* There are thousands of cultivated varieties of apples, as well as countless wild ("Johnny Appleseed" types) and crab types. Apples are among the most fragrant of the temperate-zone fruits.

(Stark Bros. Nurseries & Orchards Co.)

In themselves, they provide an exciting variety of smells and moods to choose from. They range from crisp, refreshing, outdoorsy, elusive (yet very *definite*), and healthy to the compelling aroma of a choice dinner wine or offer seemingly endless opportunities for you to overjoy (and baffle) both friends and customers with your very own unique items.

Of course, the simplest way to "deodorize" your home with their so-special so-natural flavors (scents) is to merely keep a bowl of this colorful fruit on your dining room table. In fact, you can't walk into a room containing apples and not detect their presence. You find yourself sniffing the air with pleasure.

Some of the most aromatic of apples are: MacIntosh, Winesap, Gravenstein, golden russet, and yellow Newton.

Apricots, *Prunus armeniaca*, add a tantalizing, appetizing essence to any potpourri. Drying apricots concentrates the essential oils and sugars. When using dried apricots in potpourris and sachets, cut them in small pieces to spread their aroma.

The grape of choice for fragrance is the Concord, *Vitis labrusca*. This highly aromatic fruit will also add color to your scented products. Do not use grapes to color soap or any other item you wish to use on your skin or hair, however. Grapes leave stains that are difficult to remove.

(Stark Bros. Nurseries & Orchards Co.)

(Stark Bros. Nurseries & Orchards Co.)

The red raspberry, *Rubus idaeus,* is the most fragrant. Latham is one of the best cultivars and is hardy in practically all parts of the country. Raspberries add an unusual fruity scent that is sure to please.

The delectable flavor of strawberries (which varies with kinds) adds a delightful zest to your finished products, no matter what cultivar you choose. Any of the fine varieties of strawberry, *Fragaria* x *ananassa,* is suitable for drying. Cut the berries up into small pieces to spread their "tasty" qualities throughout the mix.

Fruit Essences

Although fruit oils can be extracted, it is seldom practical to do so. For perfumes, you can capture fruit oils by preparing a tincture consisting of 1 part fruit to 6 parts alcohol.

Note: If the essence will later be used in anything *edible,* use deodorized brandy. Leave the brandy odor in the fruit if the fruit is the same or very similar to the scent you hope to achieve, for example, apricot brandy with apricot essence.

Citrus Fruits

Northerners will need to culture potted plants of citrus fruits or shop at their grocery store, to get the citrus fruits they want. If you live in an area where citrus grows outdoors, you might wish to grow your own.

All citrus are fragrant, from their flowers to their fruits. You might wish to make perfumes out of orange blossoms, for example. With citrus, the peel of the fruit contains the most oil, and hence the most fragrance. For

51

sachets and potpourris, you can dry and shred the peels. For perfumes and soaps, you will want to use the oil or prepare a tincture to extract the fragrant oils.

Orange is *Citrus sinensis*. Orange blossoms make a heavenly perfume, which might explain its popularity at weddings. Orange peel can be mixed with a few spices to provide the fragrance for aftershaves.

Grapefruit, *Citrus paradisi*, is rarely used for its aroma, but it is a stimulating and refreshing change from the lemon scents so prevalent.

Lime is *Citrus aurantifolia*. Men who are too "timid" for floral scents will find lime cologne invigorating.

Lemon, *Citrus limon*, is probably one of the most popular scents in America. It can be found in everything from dishwashing detergent to furniture polish. It is a clean and stimulating fragrance that is sure to please.

Tangerine, *Citrus nobilis deliciosa*, is another member of the citrus family that is underused. It has a distinctive tang and is an ideal citrus substitute for those weary of lemon or lime scents.

Other Tropical and Subtropical Fruits

Many of the following fruits also can be grown in the same areas as citrus.

Bananas, *Musa paradisiaca sapientum*, contrary to popular belief, do not grow on trees. The banana is a large treelike herbaceous plant with a perennial root (or rhizome). It has an annual cane (or trunk) which dies shortly after producing the fruit. New trunks rise from sprouts on the rhizome. A fully grown plant can rise as tall as 40 feet.

Both the fruit and the peel can be used to provide typical banana fragrance. The dried fruits have a longer shelf life than the peel, and are usually used.

Papaya, *Carica papaya*, is a melonlike fruit with a deep, unmistakable fragrance when ripe. It grows on small trees native to Mexico and central America. Cultivated trees can reach as high as 25 feet, but most papaya trees growing in the wild rarely exceed 6 feet in height.

The best places in the United States to grow pineapple, *Ananas comosus*, are where frost does not occur, such as south Florida and Hawaii. This golden gem of a fruit is sure to please anyone's nostrils.

Coconut, *Cocos nucifera*, although not really a fruit, is included here because of its aromatic qualities. Its generous oils almost command its use in soap and other scented products. Coconut soap is very gentle to the skin.

The olive, *Olea europaea*, also can be grown for its oils. Olive oil is the secret ingredient of castille soap, which is the standard of beauty soaps.

Spices

Most fruits lend themselves well to blending with spices. Spices, when used gingerly, can really enhance the fruit aromas. Be careful to not drown your fruits with spices, however. Some people add so many spices to apples that you cannot appreciate the natural tantalizing aroma of the apple.

Recipes with Fruits and Spices

PINA COLADA POTPOURRI
4 ounces dried pineapple (chopped)
2 ounces dried coconut (shredded)
8 ounces dried petunia or chrysanthemum blossoms
1 ounce powdered benzoin gum

TROPICAL MIX POTPOURRI
3 ounces dried banana cut into small pieces
2 ounces shredded coconut
2 ounces dried pineapple (chopped)
2 ounces papaya (dried and chopped)
2 tablespoons salt
1 tablespoon shredded tangerine peel
1 ounce balsam Peru

ORANGE POTPOURRI
8 ounces dried orange blossoms
4 ounces shredded orange peel
1 teaspoon cloves
2 tablespoons salt
1 ounce benzoin powder
2 ounces dried bee balm blossoms or 1 drop oil of bergamot

APPLE POTPOURRI
8 ounces dried apples (chopped)
8 ounces dried petunia blossoms
2 ounces dried dandelion or chrysanthemum blossoms
1 tablespoon salt
1 teaspoon cinnamon
¼ teaspoon cloves
¼ teaspoon nutmeg
¼ teaspoon ginger
1 ounce orris root powder

CITRUS SACHET
8 ounces dried orange blossoms
2 ounces shredded tangerine peel
2 ounces shredded lemon peel
1 ounce shredded orange peel
2 ounces shredded lime peel
2 ounces shredded grapefruit peel
4 ounces dried bee balm blossoms or 2 drops oil of bergamot
1 ounce powdered orris root

APPLES AND ORANGES SACHET
4 ounces dried orange blossoms
2 ounces dried apples (chopped)
1 ounce dried jasmine blossoms
2 ounces talcum powder (unscented)
1 ounce cornstarch
2 tablespoons salt
1 ounce shredded orange peel
1 teaspoon cinnamon
1 teaspoon cloves
½ teaspoon nutmeg
1 ounce Orris root powder

STRAWBERRY POTPOURRI
4 ounces dried strawberries (chopped)
8 ounces dried petunia blossoms: half red petals, half white
2 ounces dried strawberry leaves
½ teaspoon cinnamon
2 tablespoons salt
1 ounce powdered benzoin gum

GRAPE POTPOURRI
8 ounces dried chrysanthemum blossoms
4 ounces dried concord grapes (cut into small pieces)
1 ounce dried violets
4 ounces rose petals
1 ounce powdered benzoin gum
1 tablespoon salt

HERBS

There are many fragrant herbs. Some are fairly easy to grow and will find a place in your garden. Other herbs have more difficult cultural habits; you might wish to purchase them.

Herbs are an important ingredient in sachets and potpourris. Fragrant varieties can be used to scent soaps, perfumes, and eau de colognes. In potpourris, herbs are rarely used alone. Usually they are added as part of a blend of fragrances.

As well as fragrance, herbs can provide bulk and substance to a potpourri. Some herbs can be used as coloring agents, such as saffron which provides a bright yellow color.

Although most herbs have some fragrances, some are more pungent than others.

Fragrant Annual Herbs

Anise, *Pimpinella anisum*, is the spice that is often added to make delightful Christmas cookies. If it reminds you of licorice, do not be surprised. Anise is often added to licorice to add to its flavor and aromatic qualities. Anise is easy to grow in the home garden, but because it is an annual, it must be sown each year.

Basil, *Ocium basilicum*, is another herb from your kitchen cupboard that you may want to add to your potpourris and other scented items.

Chamomile, *Anthemis tinctoria*, is ideal for soap. It can also be made into a tea and used for hair rinses. It imparts beautifying qualities to hair.

The oil of the herb perilla, *Perilla frutescens*, is useful for many items, including homemade soaps.

Fragrant Perennial Herbs

With minimum care, perennial herbs come up year after year. They are a wise investment for anyone interested in a permanent garden. Plan your herb garden to include some of the following fragrant perennial herbs.

Wintergreen, *Gaultheria procumbens*, is a creeping herb, often found growing wild in the woods. It is a mouth-watering favorite for sachets.

Spearmint, *Mentha* x *spica*, will be a delightful addition to any mix. It can be combined with peppermint, *Mentha* x *piperita*, or used alone. Peppermint is an old-time favorite; however, you might need to use it sparingly to keep it from stealing the show.

Other Herbs

Balm, *Melissa officinalis*.
Fennel, *Foeniculum vulgare*.
Hops, *Humulus lupulus*.
Horehound, *Marrubium vulgare*.
Hyssop, *Hyssopus officinalis*.
Lovage, *Levisticum officinale*.
Pennyroyal, *Mentha pulegium*.
Rosemary, *Rosmarinus officinalis*.
Sage, *Salvia officinalis*.
Soapwort, *Saponaria officinalis*, is also called bouncing bet.
   It is popular for use in homemade soaps.
Tansy, *Tanacetum vulgare*.
Tea, *Camellila sinensis*.
Thyme, *Thymus vulgaris* is reminescent of when
   cough syrup was good-tasting and naturally flavored.

Recipes with Herbs

PEPPERMINT POTPOURRI
4 ounces dried peppermint leaves or 2 drops peppermint oil
1 ounce dried sweet woodruff
4 ounces dried chrysanthemum petals
1 ounce powdered balsam Tolu

HOPS POTPOURRI
4 ounces dried hops
2 ounces shredded orange peel
1 ounce benzoin gum powder
1 tablespoon celery seed powder
2 ounces dried catnip
2 ounces dried passion flower
1 tablespoon salt

ANISE POTPOURRI
4 ounces dried anise leaves or 1 tbsp. anise powder
4 ounces dried petunia blossoms
1 teaspoon licorice powder
1 tablespoon salt
1 ounce balsam Tolu

BERGAMOT POTPOURRI
4 ounces dried bee balm blossoms or 2 drops oil of bergamot
8 ounces dried petunia flowers
1 tablespoon shredded grapefruit peel
1 ounce black (orange pekoe) tea
1 tablespoon salt
1 ounce powdered balsam Peru

BERGAMOT SACHET
2 ounces unscented talcum powder
9 ounces cornstarch
1 ounce benzoin gum powder
4 ounces bee balm blossoms or 3 drops oil of bergamot
1 ounce shredded grapefruit peel

WINTERGREEN SACHET
2 ounces unscented talcum powder
9 ounces cornstarch
1 ounce benzoin gum powder
4 ounces dried wintergreen leaves or 3 drops oil of wintergreen

CHAMOMILE HAIR RINSE
4 ounces distilled water
1 ounce glycerin
8 ounces chamomile tea (dilute as desired).
   Let the tea steep, then remove the liquid from the dregs.
1 ounce coconut oil
1 ounce powdered orris root
3 drops tincture of violet or rose

Mixing Herbs

There is almost no limit to the unique and lovely scents you can create by blending herbs. Some herbs you will want to use alone; others in combination.

Herbs are usually given a back seat to the floral scents. While flowers such as roses and violets are favorites, herbs too, can be appealing. They can add a woodsy, refreshing, homey, or tangy touch to your scented products.

Many herbs that you use in your everyday cooking will likely be favorites in your potpourris. These are the aromatic ones with those special fragrances that make them so dear, just as a dab of vanilla extract behind the ears was an enticing perfume in the days of yesteryear.

Herbs, like spices, can be used sparingly. Those with the strongest smell should be used in a more sparing manner than those with lesser aroma. Strongly scented herbs will not require as many spices as the less-scented ones.

For the best selection of herbs, check the catalogs from one of the companies that specialize in herbs. (See Appendix). These companies offer a wider selection than is available in most stores. It also might not be convenient to grow everything at home. By purchasing a few of the herbs from other sources, you will have no problem meeting your needs, yet still have your own for enjoying fresh tidbits in your cooking, salads, or other dishes.

Herbal Coloring Agents

You can use various herbs to provide color to your scented products:
YELLOW—flowers of saffron or annatto seed.
VIOLET—indigo.
RED—henna.
TAN—chamomile.
GREEN—tincture of grass.
   To create various shades, dilute amounts of the coloring agent or combine coloring agents.
BLACK—indigo and henna.
PINK—dilute henna.
BROWN—henna and chamomile.

Use your imagination to create the colors that you want. Remember that when using herbal or vegetable color dyes, you will not have the bright uniform tones that come with the coal tar dyes. Rather you will have more pastel and organic-looking products.

If color is critical to your product and you do not feel content with the vegetable dyes, use commercial food dyes. They are available at most grocery stores. Directions for their use are on the labels.

Do not use other dyes in your products, especially soaps. Clothing dyes, for example, are much harsher and can cause allergic reactions, blindness, or other skin problems. You would do wise to stick to the gentle colors of nature.

Part 3
How Tos
&
More
Recipes

Chapter 5

Drying Flowers and Making Bouquets

FLORAL SCENT lies in minute quantities of volatile oils. The secret to drying flowers is to remove most of the moisture, but not the essential floral oils.

DRYING FLOWERS

There are many different ways to dry flowers—some easy, others more complicated. Whatever method you choose, select the one that best meets your particular needs, budget, and abilities.

Solar

You can dry flowers in the sun. This is the oldest natural method of drying plants. It is very easy to do and is only a matter of time, patience, and a few precautions to protect the flowers from wind, rain, and insects.

If you are drying flowers outdoors, cover them with screen or plastic to protect them from insect damage and rains. You can leave them out overnight if there is some protection from early morning dews. If the flowers get wet, they might rot.

You must also protect flowers from pets, wildlife (squirrels, chipmunks, birds) and neighborhood animals. Animals might severely damage the flowers, or even pick them up and carry them off somewhere. Birds will feed upon the seeds.

Indoors

You also can dry flowers by the solar method indoors. Place them in a sunny window or area where they will get intense sunlight for long periods of the day.

Indoor drying has many advantages:

- ❀ There is no wind to blow them away.
- ❀ There is no rain, dew, frosts, snow, or hail.
- ❀ Indoor air is almost always much drier than outside air, so the flowers will dry at a faster rate.

You will need to take precautions for indoor drying as well. First, you must be sure that you place the flowers in a window that is not too cold. Flowers set on a cold windowsill will wilt before they dry, or might simply wilt and die first. Such flowers do not make a good bouquet.

Second, household pets are likely menaces. Cats are especially curious, but puppies and even adult dogs can become intrigued watching you fuss with your flowers. Keep all animals, as well as young children, away from your flowers.

Conventional Ovens. Conventional ovens are fast and efficient ways to dry flowers. Any home gas or electric oven can be used. If you use a gas stove, you can dry flowers in the oven with the pilot light alone, or at a faster rate when set at very low heat. Electric ovens do not have pilot lights, and so must be set at their lowest temperatures. Set the flowers to be dried in a tray in the oven and leave them in for about one-half hour. Check to see how the flowers are doing. If they are starting to dry, turn the oven off and leave the oven door closed. The flowers will dry further from the heat remaining in the oven.

Salt absorbs moisture and can be used to aid in the drying process. Remember that some flowers dry faster than others. Some flowers might dry in an hour or less, whereas most flowers will take several hours or all day to dry.

Microwaves must not be used. They will not dry flowers; they will bake them. Flowers that are dried too quickly or baked might suffer damage to the plant membranes, causing a loss of volatile oils. Remember, the goal is to remove the moisture, not the oils, from the flower.

Silica Gel. Commercial florists use silica gel to preserve flowers in their whole form when drying them. Various powders are available. Silica gel performs very similarly to salt in that it absorbs moisture. It also helps to hold the form of the flower blossom, and it seals in the floral oils.

Unscented Hair Spray. If you do not object to chemicals, you can use unscented hair spray to help keep a floral bouquet. Its main effect is to "shellac" the flower so that it does not decompose when touched. This is important because dried flowers are extremely fragile. As anyone can tell you, they fall apart quite readily when handled. Even the gentlest touch can cause damage.

The brand of hair spray you use is not important, provided that it is unscented and you use it sparingly to help hold the flowers in place. Any perfume, of course, would fight with your own mix. The goal is to preserve the flowers in the best way possible.

Fruit and Vegetable Dehydrators. There are many excellent machines on the market for making fruit and vegetable leathers and flakes. If you already own one of these machines, you can also use it to dry your flowers. These machines might not be practical for drying whole flowers because most have chambers that are too small. They do work nicely for drying flowers for potpourris and sachets, though.

Dehydrators are very easy to use and come with a set of operating instructions. Always follow the instructions given by the manufacturer of the product that you are using. If the product says you cannot use it for some purpose, do not attempt that purpose.

If you do not own a dehydrator, you can use one of the cheaper methods of dehydrating flowers. Of course, if you have a lot of fruits and vegetables that you want to preserve, as well as flowers for potpourris, you might find it worthwhile to invest in such a machine.

Paper Bags. You can dry flowers by placing them in a paper (not plastic) bag and hanging it on the clothesline. Do not use plastic bags. They will not allow the moisture to escape, and they might cause heat buildup. The flowers might wilt and ferment, rather than dry.

When using paper bags, do not leave them out in the rain because the flowers inside won't dry. Rotted flowers do not make nice bouquets. You can sprinkle salt into the bags to help absorb the excess moisture.

MAKING BOUQUETS

Although you can cut and dry almost any flower for winter bouquets, some flowers are better suited for the purpose. The easiest flowers to use are those classified as *everlastings*.

Strictly speaking, everlastings do not all belong to the same species. They come in a wide variety of shapes and colors. What they all share in common is the fact that they can retain much of their color and form after they are dried. Because of these lasting qualities, they are ideally suited for winter bouquets.

People who like to have flowers on their table all year around will appreciate these inexpensive and durable flowers and the lovely arrangements and bouquets that can be made from them.

Following is a list of some of the best everlastings:

Chinese lantern Plant, *Physalis alkekengi*
Globe amaranth, *Gomphrena globsa*
Heaven bells, *Statice sinuata*
Pearly everlasting, *Anaphalis margaritacea*

Sea holly, *Eryngium maritimum*
Strawflower, *Helichrysum bracteatum*
Sunray, *Helipterum manglesii*
Winged everlasting, *Ammobium alatum*
Wood rose, *Rosa gymnocarpa*

There are other flowers used as everlastings as well, but these are among the best.

Preparing Everlastings

Everlastings are very easy to dry. Like all flowers, however, they must be prepared carefully in order to be preserved in their most comely form.

The first step in this procedure is to cut the flower stems before the flower bud has completely opened. Do not cut the flower stems while the flower buds are closed in a tight head, or they might never open. If you cut the stems when the flowers are completely open, they will not last as long, nor present as attractive a display. So cut the stems before the flower buds are fully open.

The second step is to remove the leaves. Gently strip all the leaves from the stems. Leaf removal makes the flowers easier to arrange, but the main reason to remove the leaves is to extend the life of the flower. The leafy materials will not dry as well as the floral heads.

The third step is to place the flowers in a position where they can dry. The flowers will naturally dry over a period of a few days if left in a place with air circulation and low moisture. Set them in a sunny window or hang them a paper bag on the clothesline, but take them in before any rain or snow.

Do not pile flowers too high on top of each other. Three high is about the limit. If you pile too many on each other, there may be adverse results. The top ones might crush and deform the lower ones, or they might build up heat levels and attract disease and decay organisms.

Incidentally, you cannot dry flowers by putting them in a vase of water. Believe it or not, a common mistake people make is to place everlastings in a vase of water (and wonder why they never dry.)

The refrigerator and freezer are two other areas where everlastings should not be kept. These environments are too moist. Flowers cannot dry under such conditions. Freezing flowers can cause permanent damage to their delicate membranes and destroy the beauty of the flower once it thaws out. In order for an everlasting to maintain its lasting quality, it must be dried first.

Dry Bouquets

In addition to plants previously discussed, the following are also quite effective, especially when used in bouquets:

Money plant, *Lunaria biennis*, is a biennial with fragrant purple or white flowers in the spring and early summer. It is noted for its peculiar fruit, which is silvery and flat once the seeds have been dispersed. These flat fruits resemble silver coins—hence the knickname "money plant." Plants grow up to 3 feet tall.

Job's tears, *Coix lacryma-jobi*, is a tall ornamental grass reaching up to 3 feet. Cut and hang stems in a cool airy place for drying. It is an annual that can add accents to your dried floral bouquets.

Quaking grass, *Briza minor*, is ideal for drying because it has a dwarf growth habit of up to only 16 inches. This annual "quakes" or shivers in the breeze.

Baby's breath, *Gypsophila elegans*, grows to 18 inches. It is more dwarf than other species with thick white cloudlike layers of flowers when in bloom. It blooms from June until frost. For pink flowers, plant *Gypsophila paniculata*, Pink Fairy.

Foxtail Millet, *Setaria italica*, is considered a weed to many farmers. It is easy to grow. This 3-foot-high ornamental grass plant bears large seed heads dark brown in color. You can dry these seed heads and add them to floral bouquets for accents.

Fragrance

Dried flowers can retain some of their natural fragrance if they are carefully prepared. For a stronger aroma, however, you can add floral oils to the dried bouquets. Your homemade perfumes will be equally as effective as floral oils.

Usually you will add floral scents that are different from the natural flower's smell; that is, fragrances from different flowers. You can prepare a tincture of the petals used in the bouquet to add to provide aroma after drying.

Put aside some of the flowers for making into a tincture. Use 6 parts of unscented alcohol to 1 part of flower blossom. Let the mixture sit overnight in a tightly closed container. Shake the jar occasionally to help the essential oils dissolve into the alcohol solution.

Make a separate tincture for each flower and label each jar. After you have made your floral bouquets, you will be able to use an eyedropper to drop a little of the tincture of fragrance upon each original flower. The tincture will greatly enhance the aromatic qualities of the dried bouquet. Be certain to use only a few drops at a time. By labeling jars, you will be able to tell which flower scents go to which flowers in the mix.

It is more effective to scent each individual flower than to mix them all together into one tincture. That way little bits of fragrances approach your nostrils from all different directions, providing a pleasing bouquet.

cinnamon ✓
frankincense ✓
Egyptian musk
Lavender
grapefruit oil
rose
gentian violet
jasmine
lemon oil.
vanilla

Chapter 6

*M*aking Potpourri

POTPOURRIS MADE FROM the flowers in your garden will be memories you will be able to treasure for a lifetime. It is not difficult to make potpourris. Most people do best by following an old recipe. As they become better acquainted with the sights and smells of various materials, they will be able to improvise their own recipes.

A *potpourri* is a mix. It usually consists of dried flowers, herbs, and spices. Although some people use potpourris and sachets interchangeably, potpourris do not have to be fragrant (although most are). They are ornamental and used as decorations around the house, on Christmas trees, and for other purposes.

Most people prefer their potpourris to combine visual stimuli—the various dried flowers, herbs, and spices—with a pleasing aroma. In a truly good potpourri, you should be able to smell a little bit of each fragrance in the blend. Even with a dominant scent, the odors must harmonize to be appealing. Select your prettiest glass jar to hold your potpourri.

One of the biggest mistakes people make is to go overboard with spices. The result is that you smother the more subtle fragrances of the mix. A light use of spices will allow you to smell the other scents and will make for a superior potpourri. Think of it as akin to baking a cake or pie. You do not want to add too many spices, or you destroy the recipe. The same is true when using a recipe to make potpourri.

Another common mistake people make is to use fresh flowers instead of dried. Fresh flowers might rot in your mix. Rotted flowers ruin a potpourri. They produce off-scents, destroying the fragrance of the mix as decay sets in. Always use dried flowers in potpourris you intend to keep for a period of time.

Familiarize yourself with the various scents surrounding you. Once you know the fragrances of individual items, you will be more adept at harmonizing them, and on the way to creating your own unique individual potpourris from your own recipes.

Creating a potpourri. Begin with dried herbs and flowers. Then add spices.

Stir ingredients well using a wooden spoon.

Pour the potpourri into the storage container. Use a funnel if necessary.

Plastic bottles are cheaper and more child-proof than glass, but not as attractive.

When you are ready to use the potpourri, check its consistency and aroma to see if it suits you.

Stir in extra ingredients if necessary.

Glass dishes make lovely containers for your display.

A POTPOURRI DISSECTED

To understand how to make a potpourri, we will examine a rose potpourri on a step-by-step basis. Follow along closely. Reread instructions to ensure understanding.

ROSE POTPOURRI RECIPE
1 pint dried rose petals, packed tightly into a Mason jar
2 tablespoons table, rock, or pickling salt
3 tablespoons brown sugar (not white sugar)
1 ounce powdered orris root
1 ounce powdered benzoin gum
1 teaspoon cinnamon
1 teaspoon cloves
2 teaspoons allspice
1 ounce cognac or fruit brandy

Mix ingredients well. Cover and let set for a few days. Shake again to disperse ingredients. It is now ready to be put into other containers.

For a more intense rose fragrance, add one drop of rose oil or a drop or two of homemade rose perfume.

PURPOSE OF INGREDIENTS

ROSE PETALS—add fragrance, color, and bulk to the mix.
SALT—absorbs excess moisture and acts as a preservative.
BROWN SUGAR—"sweetens" the mix and acts as a preservative.
BENZOIN GUM—stimulates the perfume of the mix and acts as a fixing
     agent to control the volatility of essential floral odors.
ORRIS ROOT—acts as a fixing agent to control the volatility of essential
     oils; adds a violetlike scent of its own which complements the bouquet.
SPICES—enhance the fragrance.
ALCOHOL—acts as a solvent. Cognac adds alcohol esters and oenanthic
     ether, which stimulate the perfume, giving it an extra-potent "zest."

FIXING AGENTS

Potpourris are easy and fun to make, and the number of varieties you can create is limited only by your imagination. All potpourris that yield fragrance must contain a fixing agent. A number of various plant gums and resins are used for this purpose, including balsam Peru, balsam Tolu, benzoin gum, orris root, sandalwood, and a few others. It is not necessary to have more than one fixing agent in each mix.

The agent that you choose will depend upon whether the other fragrant qualities of the agent itself is desired. For example, orris root smells like violets and can even be used to make an imitation violet perfume.

Note: Some people like to add vanilla extract to their potpourris. If you wish to add vanilla, 1 or 2 teaspoons is sufficient for most mixes.

76

POTPOURRI RECIPES

LILAC POTPOURRI
1 pint dried lilac flowers
2 tablespoons salt
1 ounce powdered orris root
½ pint dried rose petals

PEONY POTPOURRI
1 pint dried peony blossoms
½ pint dried rose petals
1 ounce powdered benzoin gum
2 tablespoons salt
2 tablespoons brown sugar
3 drops tincture of peony

BALSAM FIR POTPOURRI
½ pint balsam fir needle
4 ounces dried sweet woodruff leaves
1 ounce dried violet blooms
1 ounce dried heather
½ ounce dried lavender flowers
2 tablespoons salt
¼ cup bee balm blossoms or 1 drop oil of bergamot
1 ounce balsam Peru

WISTERIA POTPOURRI
1 pint wisteria blossoms, dried
1 ounce powdered balsam Tolu
½ pint dried lilac blossoms
¼ pint (4 ounces) dried rose petals
3 drops tincture of wisteria

LILY OF THE VALLEY POTPOURRI
½ pint dried lily of the valley petals
1 pint dried petunia blossoms
4 ounces dried rose blossoms
1 teaspoon vanilla extract
1 ounce orris root powder

LILY OF THE VALLEY SACHET
Add 2 ounces of unscented talcum powder, and 9 ounces of cornstarch
to the recipe for lily of the valley potpourri.

TINCTURE OF PEONY

Crush three peony blossoms into a quart Mason jar. Use only the fresh blossoms for greatest fragrance. Pack it in tightly. Add unscented alcohol up to the jar top with about 2 inches of space left. Add cognac so that the liquid covers the solid matter. Cover the jar with a tight lid. Tape it so that it will not leak. Shake the mixture thoroughly and let it sit overnight, occasionally shaking the mix.

Upon awakening, shake the jar thoroughly before opening the seal. Drain the liquid into a bottle with a tight seal. The liquid solution is the tincture. It will be colored and contain the volatile essential oils and color pigments of the blossoms. You can dry the blossoms remaining in the jar for potpourris or throw them away, as you choose.

CARNATION POTPOURRI
1 pint carnations
½ pint chrysanthemums (to add color and bulk to the mix)
1 tablespoon salt
1 teaspoon cloves
1 ounce powdered benzoin gum

The kinds of flowers used depend upon the color and texture you want, as well as the fragrance. Chrysanthemums are excellent for adding bulk, and because the petals resemble carnations, they blend right in. If you desire a red potpourri, use red flowers. The same goes for any other color you have preference for.

Chapter 7
Making Sachets

YOU CAN PLACE a bar of heavily perfumed soap in a clothes drawer for use as a sachet. You also can make a number of sachets merely by slicing up the soap and enclosing it in little pillowlike bags.

Sachets differ from potpourris in many ways, yet are very similar in others. Often, people find it hard to distinguish between the two. Think of potpourri as flowers in a glass jar and sachet as little scented pillows.

Sachets are usually enclosed in little cloth bags called *sachet pillows* or just *sachets*. Most often they are powdered mixes more finely ground than potpourris. Although they tend to have a floral dominance and fewer spices than potpourris, sachets can be made from many ingredients very similar to potpourris. Pine needles for example, can be ground up to make sachets, as can balsam fir needles for outdoor scents.

Although ingredients do not need to be ground into a powder, most are. Pine needles would spear through the fabric, tearing it, if they were not ground into smaller pieces.

HOW TO MAKE SACHETS

To make sachets, cut pieces of suitable cloth into rectangles. Sew the cloth pieces, one on top of the other, on three sides so that only one side is open. Turn the pillow inside out, so that the stitches are on the inside.

Fill the pillow one-half to three-fourths full with the sachet powder. Do not fill it entirely full or you will have difficulty sewing up the open end.

Sew the open end. The pillows must be sewn together tightly. No sachet powder should be able to leak out.

For cloths with large open weaves, you might need to sew an inner pillow and use the other fabric as a decorative cover.

You can use embroidery to embellish pillows, or you can use special cloth paints that are designed to simulate embroidery. They do not look as impressive as embroidery, but are easier for people who lack either embroidery skills or time.

Plain white cloth is often used for sachets, but you can use colored fabrics, as well. If you are using odds and ends for fabric material, remember it is best to use only those fabrics made from natural fibers.

It is often a good idea to write the year on each pillow so you can remember what year it was made. It helps to know how long the sachets are lasting. Again, this is an option you might or might not wish to pursue.

Sometimes people write the name of the sachet onto each pillow in a small corner. This practice will not be necessary once you become more familiar with the various scents, but is okay for the novice. You can add your name if you like, and use lace to cover up such markings.

Alternate Method

You can make sachet pillows in any size. Even if you do not know how or have time to sew, you can make a sachet. Take a square sheet of linen or other suitable cloth.

Fold in the four corners to form a cloth bag. Be certain that each corner is included. Fill the bag about one-half full with sachet powder.

Hold the bag with one hand, and you use your free hand to tie a colorful ribbon around its neck. Tie tightly so that sachet powder will not escape. Tie the ribbon into an attractive bow, if you like.

Voila—instant sachet! You might wish to put a rubberband around the container beneath the ribbon, to make it more secure.

Common Mistakes

When filling the sachet pillows, be careful not to overfill them. It is difficult to sew the pillows if they are stuffed too full, and there is a greater likelihood of their leaking.

Remember to turn the pillow inside out after sewing the first three sides. That way you hide the stitches, and make the container more leakproof.

1. Take a suitable piece of cloth.

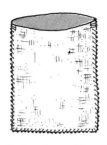

2. Sew three sides of . the fabric, leaving only one side open.

3. Turn the pillow inside out. Pour the sachet powder into the pillow until it is one-half to three-fourths full. Leave room to sew the top.

How To Make Sachets.

4. Sew the top of the pillow so no sachet powder can escape.

Alternate Method.

1. Take a suitable piece of cloth.

2. Fold the cloth into a little bag.

3. With one hand hold the bag. Loosen your grip and pour the sachet powder slowly into the bag until it is half full.

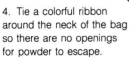

4. Tie a colorful ribbon around the neck of the bag so there are no openings for powder to escape.

5. Tie the ribbon into a bow for an attractive touch.

Threads located inside a sachet are less subject to stress and breakage than those that are exposed. Exposed threads can easily become tangled or caught in something. They are also tempting to pets, and even your friends, who always seem fascinated by loose threads. If threads are allowed to unravel, the pillow will be destroyed.

Sachets are used to impart their fragrance in chests of drawers, closets, towels, bed sheets, and more. The most common way to make sachet powders is in a base of starch mixed with small quantities of unscented talc. Cornstarch is most frequently used, but rice or potato starch also can be used. Recipes will vary slightly in the ratio of starch to talcum powder, but talc should not exceed one-fourth of the base ingredients.

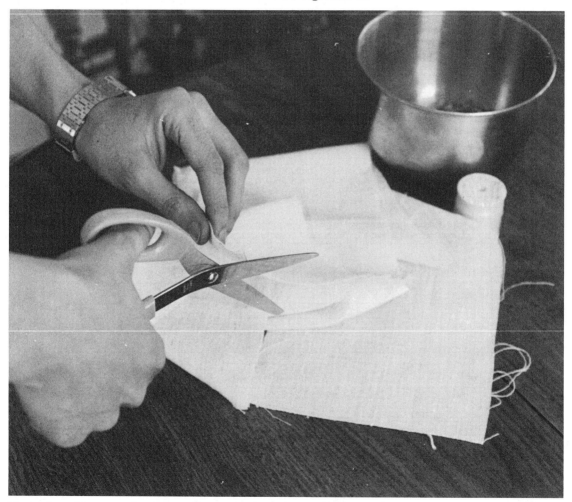

To make a homemade sachet, first cut a breathable fabric into a square of the size you desire.

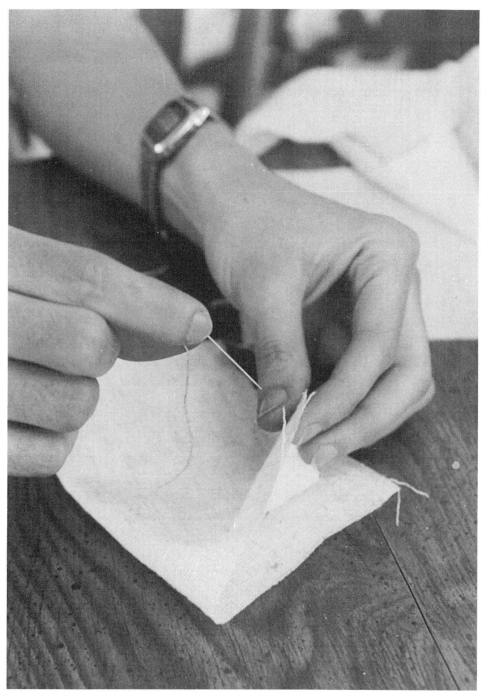

If you are using several bags of cloth, sew the corners together, then sew three sides of the packet together.

If you are using the alternate method, cut the square of fabric. Then cut the ribbon.

Next pour the sachet into the center of the cloth.

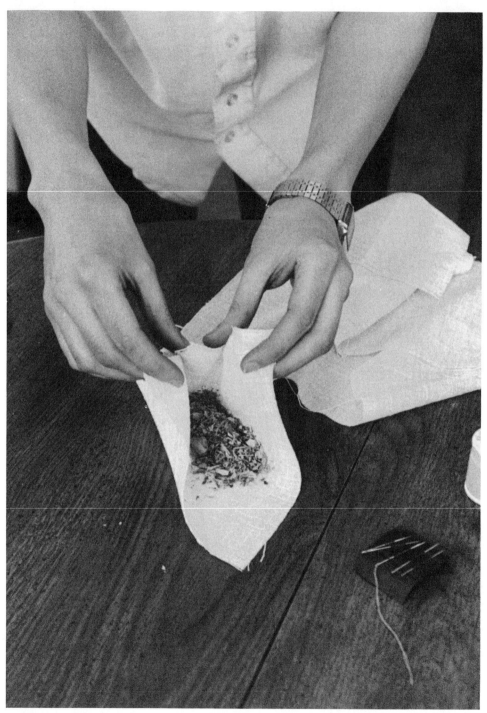

Fold the corners of the cloth together as shown.

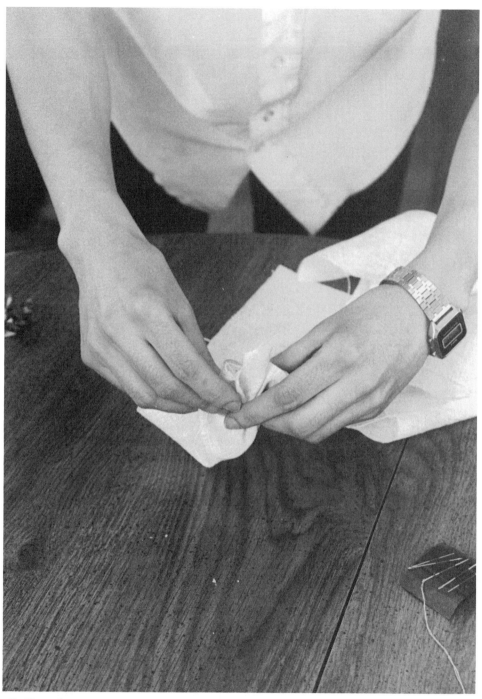

Gather the corners together. You can use thread to secure the corners before you add the ribbon.

Finally, tie a decorative ribbon around the corners of the sachet.

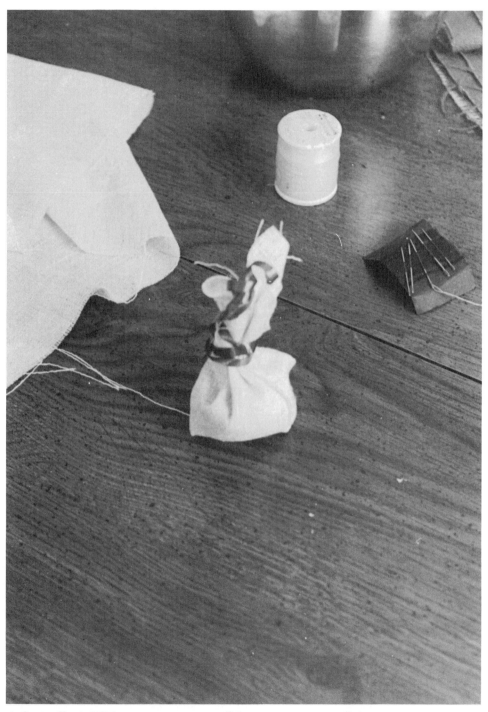

A first effort. With practice, you will become more proficient.

You can make other packets from different materials and colorful fabrics for variety or to match your decor.

A white lace sachet pillow with a colorful silk ribbon makes a nice Christmas gift.

Lace-covered potpourris. (Country Treasures)

FIXING AGENTS

Like perfumes, sachets need a fixing agent to stabilize the volatile fragrant oils in the mix. Without such an ingredient, these oils would rapidly evaporate, and the sachet would lose its fragrance.

The fixing agents used for sachets are often the same as for perfumes. Basically, they are resins and gums. Some which can be used as fixing agents in sachets, such as frankincense and myrhh, are usually not used in perfumes, because of their strong scents. Alcohol is rarely used in sachets.

Fixing agents for sachets include benzoin gum, balsam Peru, balsam Tolu, orris root, frankincense, myrhh, and sandalwood.

Benzoin and balsam Peru are perhaps the best fixing agents. Orris root is very effective at absorbing odors and releasing them, but it has a strong fragrance of its own, which resembles violets. In fact, an artificial violet perfume can be made with orris root providing the fragrance. Bergamot oil and glycerin also can be used in minute amounts to help stabilize odors. Bergamot has a slight, interesting essence.

Frankincense and myrhh also have their own scents, although not as strong in a sachet as in a perfume. Myrhh has a heavy odor. Some people think it conflicts with the lighter fragrance of most flowers.

SACHET RECIPES

Sachet powders are easy and economical to prepare. Frequently sachets have more emphasis on floral scents than potpourris. This need not always be true, however. You can make sachets with herbs or other aromatic plant material.

The strongest scented sachets call for floral oils (or perfume) as an ingredient. You also can make them from dried flowers, however. You can add homemade perfumes (see Chapter 9) as a last ingredient to give your sachets extra potency, if you wish, or to substitute for expensive floral oils.

ROSE SACHET
9 ounces cornstarch
2 ounces talcum powder (unscented)
1 ounce powdered balsam Peru
4 ounces dried rose petals or 3 drops rose oil
1 tablespoon salt

VIOLET SACHET
9 ounces cornstarch
2 ounces unscented talcum powder
1 ounce powdered orris root
1 tablespoon salt
4 ounces dried violet blossoms or 3 drops oil of violet

IMITATION VIOLET SACHET
8 ounces cornstarch
2 ounces unscented talcum powder
1 tablespoon salt
3 ounces powdered orris root
2 ounces dried jasmine petals
2 ounces dried rose blossoms

LAVENDER SACHET
8 ounces potato starch
2 ounces unscented talcum powder
1 tablespoon salt
½ ounce orris root powder
1 ounce benzoin gum powder
4 ounces lavender dried blossoms or 3 drops oil of lavender

LEMON SACHET
2 ounces shredded lemon peel
1 ounce dried bee balm blossoms or 1 drop oil of bergamot
2 ounces unscented talcum powder
8 ounces cornstarch
1 ounce balsam Peru

SUMMER SACHET
1 ounce balsam fir needles
2 ounces sweet woodruff
2 ounces bee blossoms or 1 drop oil of bergamot
1 ounce violet blossoms
2 ounces unscented talcum powder
8 ounces cornstarch
1 ounce benzoin gum powder

HELIOTROPE SACHET
4 ounces dried heliotrope petals
2 ounces dried rose petals
1 ounce dried jasmine
1 ounce benzoin gum powder
2 ounces unscented talcum powder
8 ounces cornstarch

STRAWBERRY SACHET
4 ounces dried strawberries, chopped
2 ounces dried rose petals
1 tablespoon salt
2 ounces unscented talcum powder
8 ounces cornstarch

CARNATION SACHET
8 ounces dried carnation flowers
1 ounce dried rose petals
1 teaspoon cloves
1 tablespoon salt
1 ounce benzoin gum powder
2 ounces unscented talcum powder
8 ounces cornstarch

SANDALWOOD SACHET
4 ounces sandalwood chips
2 ounces unscented talcum powder
8 ounces cornstarch

CEDARWOOD SACHET
4 ounces cedarwood chips
2 ounces unscented talcum powder
8 ounces cornstarch
1 tablespoon salt
1 ounce benzoin gum powder

LILAC SACHET
4 ounces dried lilacs
2 ounces dried rose petals
2 ounces unscented talcum powder
8 ounces cornstarch
1 ounce balsam Peru

FLORAL BOUQUET SACHET
2 ounces dried carnations
2 ounces dried rose petals
2 ounces dried violet blossoms
4 ounces dried lilac blooms
1 ounce benzoin gum powder
1 tablespoon salt
3 ounces unscented talcum powder
10 ounces cornstarch

Chapter 8

Soap, Candles, Bubble Baths, and Shampoos

IN DAYS OF YESTERYEAR making your own soap and candles was an event that usually involved the whole family. People would get together, sometimes whole neighborhoods, to produce a huge batch of soap and candleware. Today, both products are so inexpensive to buy that the art of making them has all but vanished. Yet, there is a special satisfaction to making your own.

Soap can be scented or unscented, as you choose. You can make everything from delicate face soaps to laundry soaps right in your kitchen. Since you control the ingredients, you will not need to worry about harmful chemical additives or the allergic reactions people with delicate complexions often get when using commercial soaps.

MAKING SOAP

You can add emolients to soap for their desirable qualities. Such ingredients include cold cream, lanolin, cocoa butter, or even powdered oatmeal. Add emolients in appropriate amounts, so as to not affect the soap-making process. Also, you should add most emolients after the soap has saponified while it is still cooling. Remember to always add fragrances as the very last ingredient.

You can also add special ingredients to soap, such as aloe vera, vitamin E, wheat germ oil, jojoba oil, vitamins A and D, and baking soda. Do not add cornstarch to soap. Cornstarch can leave a thin film on your skin that might attract bacteria. Do not put in your soap any ingredients that might be poisonous. Poisons can be absorbed through the skin.

Some people like to add buttermilk (in liquid or powder form) to their homemade soaps; others like to add lemon juice. Coconut oil is a favorite ingredient for people who really like suds.

Do not add any ingredient that you are allergic to unless you do not plan to use the soap yourself.

Ingredients

There are only three ingredients essential to making soap: grease (fat), lye, and water. Other ingredients are added to give certain desired qualities to the soap.

Although soap making is fairly simple to do, it is critical that you follow instructions carefully. Lye is a caustic substance. If mishandled, it can burn skin or even cause blindness. Add lye only to *cold water.* Never add lye to hot water, because it might cause a violent chemical reaction.

Most commercial lye is either a caustic soda, such as sodium hydroxide, or a mineral salt known as potassium hydroxide. Hard soaps are made with sodium hydroxide or caustic soda; soft soaps are made with potassium hydroxide.

Most ingredients for making soaps can be found in your kitchen.

Lye is commercially available with instructions for its use on the can. You also can make your own lye water by soaking a bucket of wood ashes overnight. The water that you pour off in the morning will be lye water. This is the way colonials made their soap.

Use only wood ashes. Do not try to make lye water from coal or coke ashes. Coal ashes contains chemicals that might irritate or damage the skin.

Some people add salt to help curdle the soap, but it is not necessary. You can add baking soda, or sodium bicarbonate, to soap. It is an inexpensive ingredient that contributes desirable qualities, including deodorizing and cleansing.

Improving Soap

Most soaps made at home will need to be improved before they are suitable for personal use. To improve soap, you might wish to remelt it and add more fats and oils. This process helps to harden soap and also makes it gentler to the skin. Naturally, you will need to keep everything in proportion. Too much oil might create a slushy, ineffective soap. The purpose of soap is to aid in removing grease and grime, not to leave a layer of grease on you, although a good soap will have a slightly oily feel to it.

You must add perfumes only *after* the soap has started to cool. Add them before the liquid soap is poured into molds, however, so that the finished bars have a uniform scent. Of course, you do not need to add fragrances to your soap if you prefer them to remain unscented.

A warm lavender bath is both refreshing and relaxing. It is particularly soothing to infants.

If you wish to color your soap, you can use a vegetable coloring. The colors will be more pastel and variable than those produced by chemical coal-tar dyes. The latter will produce uniform colors of a brighter hue. If you want bright colors, you can use food dyes. Be careful to not add so much color that it comes off as you wash, however.

Equipment

Your eyes are your most important body organ. Do not risk losing them. Goggles or hard eyeglasses are a wise investment. Some eye protection is desirable to protect eyes from lye fumes. It is better to be safe than sorry, or worse yet, blind! Protect your eyes before you begin to make soap.

Rubber gloves will offer great protection from any accidental splashes of lye onto the hands. Lye is extremely caustic and can burn skin, so be extremely careful when handling it. Once a chemical reaction called *saponifiction* has taken place, the material will not be as caustic.

Wear a long-sleeved shirt or blouse, long pants, and hard shoes. Do not make soap in your shorts or bare feet.

After you have equipped yourself with safety gear, you will need some equipment for the process itself.

A large kettle and a large wooden spoon are critical. Do not attempt to make soap in a small pan; use a large kettle. A large wooden spoon will be handy for stirring. Wood is preferable to metal because the handle will not conduct heat as rapidly. A metal spoon will quickly become too hot to touch.

Be sure to use a large spoon. A small spoon could easily slip out of your hand and into the hot mixture. Retrieving it would be a very risky task.

A small spoon also puts your hand much too close to the hot mixture. A large spoon gives you the convenience of distance and safety.

A measuring cup is very practical for measuring out the ingredients. While you do not have to be exact as in a cake recipe, you still need to have some idea of the proportions that you are using. A successful recipe requires you to measure ingredients. "By guess and by golly" could mean a big mess and a tragic waste of time, money, and materials.

You need not buy special soap molds. Although they are available, you can use almost any shallow pan for making soap. Cupcake tins are ideal. They form nice, round cakes of soap that don't require cutting. Fill them up to half full.

Homemade soap can be shaped in many forms. Round balls are easy to make.

You also can use a large rectangular metal pan. Shallow pans are preferable to deep-dish pans for soap molds. For one thing, the soap will be easier to remove from a shallow pan. Also, it will form a shape that is more in keeping with the standard size of cakes that you are familiar with. You will probably not want soap in one- or two-pound blocks.

You will want to keep the pans and dishes you use for soap making separate from your regular cooking pans. If you do decide to use them in cooking, soak them completely immersed in hot water several times first. Then apply the "sniff and feel" test to be sure that there's not even a hint of soap left on them.

How Soap is Made

When grease and lye are heated together, a chemical reaction called saponification occurs. The resulting product is soap. To put it in simpler terms, soap is made by a boiling process. Cold water, lye, and grease—your choice of hydrogenated vegetable oils (like Crisco), tallow, or lard—are heated and boiled. Liquid vegetable oils also may be used. Once the mixture thickens to a gravylike texture, it is saponified and needs to be removed from the heat and cooled.

Saponification is the chemical reaction that takes place in the boiling process of soap making. What occurs is chemically complex. Simple fats do not combine with the alkali (lye) to form soap. First, they decompose (water acts as a solvent base) into fatty acids and glycerols, which then combine, forming soap.

Pour the hot liquid into the molds before it has completely cooled. Do not let it cool too long in the pan. Soap hardens as it cools. If left in the pan, it will completely harden into one giant glob of soap, something you will not want.

Cut the soap into similarly shaped bars after you have poured it into a shallow pan. You should use a wire to cut the soap because it will be able to cut the soap evenly and make attractive cakes of similar width and length. Do not use a knife, or you might have bars that are not equal in appearance. You want people to be impressed by your homemade soaps, not to laugh at you.

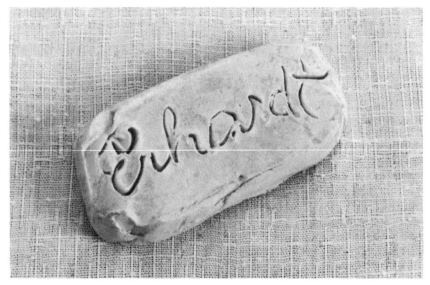

Cut the soap into cakes before it has completely hardened. If you wait until after the soap has set and is hard, it will be very difficult to cut. Hard soap does not cut easily, as you can test for yourself with a bar of ordinary soap you have on hand. It splinters and forms a mess. Cut the soap while it is still pliable, just before it hardens, and it will retain its shape.

Cut the soap into cakes before it hardens.

Soap making is easy, but it requires concentration to detail. Children and pets should not be present when soap is being made. They are too distracting and likely to be unaware of the serious hazards involved in making soap. Lock the doors and keep them out of the room when making soap. If necessary, hire a babysitter, or drop the kids and pets off with mom and dad.

Be sure that there are no other distractions while you make your soap. Take the telephone off the hook and turn off the television and radio. You must give your total attention to the task at hand. That is the only safe and practical way to make soap.

There are no special skills required to make soap. However, you must follow instructions for success and for safety's sake.

A Shortcut to Soap Making

If you do not wish to handle lye, do not have wood ashes available, or do not have the time to make soap from scratch, you can still make homemade soaps. You can purchase castille granules at most drugstores. There is no need to mess with lye when using these granules. Since they are actually granulated soap, it is easy to make soap from them.

Put the granules into a kettle and add water. Instructions for use will probably be on the package. If not, use common sense in adding water. (Don't drown the granules.)

Heat the mixture at low to medium heat and stir it constantly with a large wooden spoon. The granules will dissolve.

Stir the mixture until it is smooth. Remove it from the heat and add any other ingredients or emolients that you want. Stir them in well as the soap cools.

Add perfume (if desired) as the very last ingredient. Blend it in so that the fragrance will be evenly dispersed.

Pour the mixture into molds, and let harden.

If the soap does not set (that is, if the bars do not get hard) reheat the mixture, adding more castille granules as necessary. Before it cools completely, you will need to add more perfume because reheating the mix will release the volatile floral oils, thus destroying them.

Recipes for Soap

WHITE ROSE TOILET SOAP

1 pound of hydrogenated vegetable oil or lard
2 ounces coconut oil
4 ounces commercial lye dissolved in cold water
1 ounce baking soda (sodium bicarbonate)
1 tablespoon salt
1 ounce glycerine
3 drops oil of rose

Place the water, lye, and grease into a large kettle on a medium flame. Stir continuously with a large wooden spoon.

The water will evaporate as the mixture thickens. The mixture will thicken and spit up like gravy, indicating that saponification has taken place.

Remove the mixture from the stove, stir it to help it cool evenly. It is important to stir the hot soap while it is heating to prevent it from scorching on the bottom of the pan.

Add the remaining ingredients, except for the perfume. Add color if desired.

Add perfume. Pour into molds.

Note: Saturated fats usually give a better performance in soap making, which is why lard and tallow were once used exclusively in this process. Hydrogenated vegetable oils, however, which are solid at room temperature, can be excellent substitutes for lard or tallow and are generally preferred by vegetarians. Liquid vegetable oils can be used, but you might need to reheat several times to get a hard soap. Unless you like the smell of peanuts, avoid using peanut oil.

CASTILLE SOAP

1 pint olive oil
4 ounces lye dissolved in cold water (follow instructions on the can)

The water evaporates as the soap thickens. Stir it constantly to prevent scorching on the bottom of the pan, which will discolor and might produce off-scents in the finished soap.

As the soap cools, add a few drops of almond extract. Color if desired. Pour into molds.

Almond oil added to Castille soap makes a wonderful skin softener.

Making Soap from Old Grease

Grease, vegetable shortening, oil, lard, or tallow—that is no longer any good for cooking can still be used to make soap. Even rancid oils, which you might ordinarily throw away, will make perfectly good soap. However, you must clean up old grease before using it to make soap.

To clean old grease, empty the grease into a large kettle. Do not try to boil grease in a pan that is too small because grease splatters when hot and can cause severe burns.

Dress appropriately for the occasion—long sleeves, long pants, leather or hard shoes—and cover hands with rubber gloves. If you have long hair, pin it up or put it in a hairnet. Protective eyewear is recommended. Either goggles or hard eyeglasses will do.

Place the kettle on the stove or electric range and turn to its highest level of heat.

Boil the grease 5 to 10 minutes. Turn off the burner and remove the kettle from the heat.

Let it cool a few minutes. Sediments will go to the bottom. Dip out the clean grease with a dipper or long-handled soup ladle. If the dipper or ladle is made of metal with a metal handle, use a pot holder when handling it so as to not burn yourself.

Remove as much of the clean grease as possible. Try to not stir up the sediments from the bottom while removing the clean grease. The clean grease will be ready for soap making.

Throw away the sediments. Do not put them into the soap.

MAKING CANDLES

The best candles are made with beeswax. Beeswax is available in most supermarkets, although you might find it expensive. It produces a bright and steady flame and burns slowly. Candles made from beeswax last longer than those made from paraffin.

Paraffin wax is also available in most supermarkets, and is usually much cheaper than beeswax. Paraffin candles produce a bright and steady flame, but the wax melts fast.

Some people combine the two waxes. They use beeswax as an outer coating over the paraffin, thus slowing down the speed at which the candle burns. This method is quite economical and practical.

Colonials made candles from tallow, much like they made soap. It is easier to make candles out of paraffin or beeswax, however. Because paraffin is already a wax, all you need do is melt it, scent and color it, and mold it in the shape desired. The addition of an outer layer of beeswax is recommended for giving candles a longer burning life.

Dipping

You can make candles using several processes. The easiest method is by dipping.

Tie several pieces of string at a uniform length to a wooden stick.

Use a wide-mouthed pot to melt the wax in. The strings should not extend beyond the pot. If they do they might catch fire.

It will take several dippings into the wax to give the strings enough coats to become candles. You must dip at the time the wax is starting to cool off. If the wax is too hot, it will dissolve the first layers of wax that you got from earlier dippings, which defeats your purpose.

Dipping is a slow process. If the wax starts to harden up you might need to reheat it slightly to get it to melt into a more pliable material so that you can work with it.

Using Molds

Another way to make candles, which is probably easier than dipping, is to use candlestick molds. You can purchase these molds in various crafts stores, or through mail-order supply houses. You also can make your own.

106

There are many sizes and shapes that candles can be made in. Most people prefer the long, narrow candles, but many of the stockier ones are coming into vogue.

To scent candles, add perfume as the last ingredient before pouring them into molds. Mix the wax thoroughly so that the fragrance has a chance to permeate the entire batch.

Making Candles by the Dipping Process.

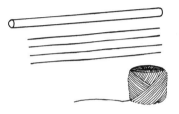

1. You will need a wooden stick and strings of equal length.

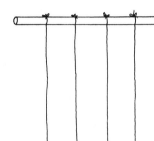

2. Tie the string to the stick. Use equal spaces between each string.

3. After the wax has been removed from the heat and has started to cool, dip the strings into the pot.

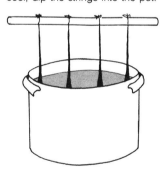

4. Several repeat dippings will be necessary. Each dipping will add a layer of wax to the previous one.

5. When the candles are the desired thickness, set the stick between two bricks until the candles finish drying.

6. When the candles are hard, untie them and clip off the extra string.

107

Materials needed to make candles: a wooden spoon, string, wax, pot, burner.

Wrap the string around the spoon and drop the wicks in the wax.

Dip slowly, so as to coat the wick with each dunk.

Let the hot wax drip into the plan. Allow the candle to cool, then repeat.

Turn the burner off so the wax starts to cool and continue to dip the candles.

If the wax cools too much, reheat it and stir if necessary.

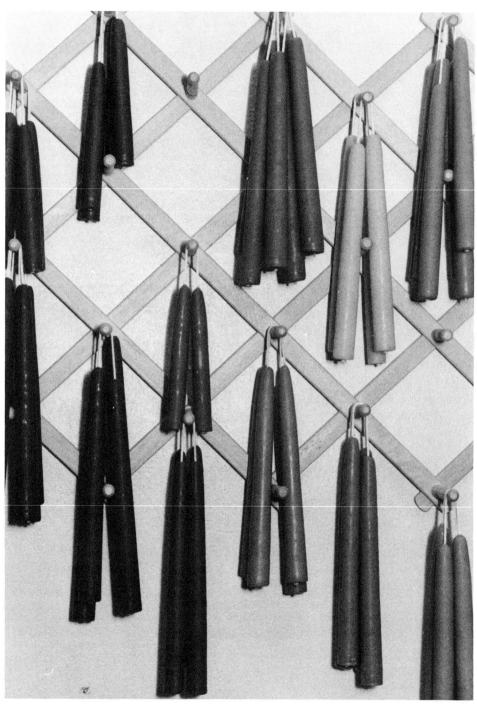

Candles should be allowed to dry. As shown, you can make them in different lengths, using longer or shorter string. (Thistledown)

MAKING BUBBLE BATH

Any good soap can be used to make bubble bath, but castille soap is generally preferred. Before the soap can be made into bubble bath it must be converted to a liquid. To do this, grate 1 bar of castille soap into 1 quart of water. (Warm water helps dissolve the soap faster.) Allow the soap and water to mix well so that you have a liquid soap solution.

There are two ingredients that can convert liquid soap into bubble bath. These ingredients can be used together or independently of each other. An old-fashioned way to make bubble bath is to add glycerine to liquid soap (soap shavings and water). Glycerine has the ability to make bubbles and increase suds. Coconut oil is often used as a substitute for glycerine, which is usually much higher priced. Coconut oil is very effective at creating lather. Both glycerine and coconut oil are known for their special skin-softening properties.

BUBBLE BATH
1 quart water
1 bar castille soap, grated or flaked
2 ounces glycerine
3 drops perfume

ROSE BUBBLE BATH
1 quart water
1 bar grated castille soap
1 ounce coconut oil
1 ounce glycerine
1 drop jasmine perfume
2 drops rose perfume

LILAC BUBBLE BATH
1 quart water
1 bar grated castille soap
3 ounces glycerine
3 drops lilac perfume

LAVENDER BUBBLE BATH
1 quart water
1 bar grated castille soap
3 ounces glycerine
4 drops lavender perfume or 2 drops lavender floral oil

VIOLET BUBBLE BATH
1 quart water
1 bar grated castille soap
2 ounces coconut oil
1 ounce glycerine
3 drops violet perfume or 2 drops violet floral oil

MAKING SHAMPOOS

Shampoos are essentially liquid soaps for washing hair. Although bar soaps can be used, most people are accustomed to using liquid soaps for shampooing and might find them easier to work with.

To make shampoo, you must have a highly concentrated liquid soap—more concentrated than would be needed for other purposes. Shampoos also can benefit from extra ingredients especially known for their beneficial properties to hair. Such ingredients include aloe vera, chamomile, comphrey, glycerine, and lanolin. You can use these ingredients alone or in combination. If you are using ingredients that are perishable, such as eggs or aloe vera, you might wish to make small batches of shampoo, to last a week, for example. Refrigeration can keep perishable products viable longer, but might not be practical, and also has its limits.

You also can add herbal coloring agents, such as henna, saffron, or others to your shampoo, or perhaps more effectively to hair conditioners.

SHAMPOO:
1 pint water
2 bars grated castille soap (or other gentle complexion soap)
1 ounce glycerine
1 ounce chamomile (tea)
3 drops perfume

BEER SHAMPOO
½ pint beer (any brand)
1 bar grated castille soap
2 ounces glycerine
1 ounce hops (tea)

EGG SHAMPOO
1 pint water
2 bars grated castille soap
1 ounce tincture of benzoin
3 egg yolks
2 ounces glycerine
3 drops perfume (desired scent)

Note: It is very important to rinse your hair thoroughly to remove all residues of shampoo. Do not use any product that has a foul odor or looks suspicious. If you are not certain how long the product has been sitting, it is best to discard it and prepare a new batch.

Chapter 9

Perfumes, Colognes, Toilet Waters, & Aftershaves

THE SECRET OF making perfumes and colognes lies in the quality of the ingredients used. French perfumes are the standard of quality in the perfume industry. Although you can make something a little cheaper by using coal-tar imitations (and sell it by the gallon), there is a noticeable difference in quality perfumes. A good perfume will linger; a bad perfume just smells up the place.

We've all had the unpleasant experience of sitting next to someone on the bus who just stinks with such an overpowering odor. Most of us know people who you can smell a half-block away. The best thing you can do is give them some natural perfume as a gift and pray that they will throw away that ghastly stuff they are presently using.

PERFUME

There are four basic components to perfume:

✿ Alcohol, which acts as a solvent, a base, and helps to release the fragrance as it evaporates.

✿ Oils, which are sometimes used to help accentuate floral oils.

✿ A fixing agent, which is essential. Fixing agents lessen the volatility of the floral oils so that all of the fragrance does not leave the bottle after one opening. It helps to stabilize the mix.

✿ Floral oils, which give perfume its fragrance.

Other ingredients usually added are distilled water and a coloring agent.

Alcohol

For perfume purposes, a high concentration of spirits (90 to 95 percent alcohol by volume) is ideal. The spirits are concentrated by a series of distillations. Unless you have a still, however, you might not be able to achieve this high a concentration of alcohol. Thus, you might want to purchase an alcohol with a high concentration of spirits. Fortunately, good-quality perfumes and excellent eau de colognes are made with lower concentrates of spirits.

Wine spirits made from grapes is the choicest alcohol for perfumes, probably because grape spirits contain traces of oenanthic ether. It is no accident that France, which is famous for its fine grape wines, is also famous for its perfumes. Wine spirits made from grapes is one of the secret ingredients of quality French perfumes.

Most sweet grape wines contain about 12 percent alcohol by volume. Vermouth, which is usually served as an appetizer wine, may contain 20 percent alcohol by volume. Sparkling wines, such as champagne, usually are only 10 to 12 percent alcohol by volume.

Many other alcohols can be used. Grain alcohols usually contain higher concentrations of spirits than do wines. Vodka, whiskey, and gin are examples of grain alcohols. Beverage alcohol is sold according to *proof*. The proof of an alcohol is equal to twice the amount of alcohol by volume it contains. For example, something that is labeled 90 proof means that it contains 45 percent alcohol by volume. Common gins are usually 90 proof. Vodka comes in 80 proof (which is 40 percent alcohol by volume) and 100 proof (50 percent alcohol). A product called bonded whiskey is 100 proof.

One of the grape wines with the highest concentrations of spirits is a French brandy called Cognac. It is usually 45 percent alcohol by volume.

French perfumes are the standard of quality in the industry.

Nonbeverage alcohols are perfectly acceptable for making perfumes. Most of these alcohols can be purchased with a higher concentration of spirits and are much cheaper than beverage alcohols. Most of these alcohols are denatured alcohol. Denatured alcohol cannot be taken internally. It contains a small amount of poisonous materials, which are added by law to ensure that the alcohol is not used for human consumption. Some alcohols, such as those made from wood, are naturally poisonous.

Rubbing alcohol, which is usually quite economical, is an example of an alcohol with a high concentration of spirits (70 percent). Because of its cost, availability, and high alcoholic content, it is ideal for making perfumes. In the case of rubbing alcohol, use only the unscented variety for making perfumes.

Caution: Do not use any perfume containing *nonbeverage* alcohol in cooking. If you wish to make perfumes that are edible and useful for flavoring cakes, cookies, candies and other confections, use only beverage alcohol, such as vodka or cognac, to provide the spirits for your perfumes.

119

Deodorizing Alcohol

Beverage alcohols that have strong scents of their own, such as whiskey, should be deodorized before using. It is very easy to deodorize beverage alcohol. Filter it through horticultural-grade charcoal to deodorize it. Use only charcoal that is labeled *horticultural grade* for this purpose. Such charcoal is readily available at most dime stores or garden centers in the plant section. Horticultural charcoal is economical and comes in bags of various sizes. A small bag should be sufficient.

Do not try to substitute any charcoal. Charcoal used for grills or stoves is not acceptable for deodorizing beverage spirits. Such charcoal might contain impurities, and charcoal made from compressed coal dust, contains harmful chemicals.

Making a charcoal filter is easy. You can use clean cloth and a jar, or coffee filters. Paper coffee filters are available at most grocery stores.

If you have any doubts as to the strength of your filters (resistance to tearage) double up the filters. Fill the filters only half full with charcoal. Do not fill them completely full or you will make a mess when you try to pour the alcohol through. Pour slowly.

If the first time you pour the alcohol through, it is slightly discolored and still smells strong, filter it again, as many times as necessary. The charcoal will rid the alcohol of the impurities, which gives it its scent.

You probably will not want to deodorize your cognac. The fruity smell of the grapes will harmonize very well with most floral odors.

Floral Oils

Natural floral oils usually cost more than chemical synthetics, but the real oils are more delicate. Many of these oils are imported from European countries, which still take pride in making perfumes the old-fashioned way: from natural flowers.

You can extract your own floral oils by gathering the petals of your favorite flowers and putting them into a jar. Fill the jar with alcohol, leaving an inch or two at the top of the jar. Add 2 tablespoons oil. Cover the jar tightly and let it sit for a few days.

The oil is essential to capture the floral oils as the alcohol releases them from the flower petals. Alcolhol acts as a solvent.

Your homemade floral oils will not be as concentrated as commercial products because a large number of petals must be gathered to produce the oil.

The alcohol will also dissolve color pigments from the flower petals, which will give color to your solution. You might want to add more color to the final perfume, or you might be content with the natural light hues.

Oils

Floral oils are usually expensive, but you can add other vegetable oils to perfumes. Oil helps to hold aromas. Minute amounts of olive oil may be added. Do not use peanut oil. Remember to use only a few drops of oil (depending upon the quantity of perfume you are making). Too much oil will make for a greasy perfume when applied to the skin or clothing.

Fixing Agents

There are two types of fixing agents: animal oils, and resins or gums. Animal oils such as musk, civet, and ambergris have their own odors that linger long after delicate floral vapors have vanished. Too much musk oil will produce a heavy perfume. For this reason, certain plant gums and resins are generally preferred. Three of the most effective are: benzoin gum, balsam Peru, and balsam Tolu.

You can also use other resins and gums, such as from sandalwood and any of those used to fix sachet aromas. Make them into a tincture before adding them to the perfume. You want all ingredients to be liquid to avoid clogging spray nozzles if using an atomizer.

Glycerin can act as a fixing agent also, because it lessens the volatility of floral oils. It is rarely used alone, however.

Preparing A Tincture

You can make tinctures by dissolving 1 part powdered gum or resin in 6 parts alcohol. Cover the container tightly. Let it set overnight. Shake the container from time to time to speed up the dissolution. Shake it once more before using. (See Appendix.)

EAU DE COLOGNE

Cologne is essentially perfumed water. It has a more delicate scent than perfume because it is not as concentrated. It also does not last as long, although a good cologne will linger for some time after it has been applied.

Use only distilled water when making cologne. Water with a high mineral content might interfere with the quality of the cologne, or add scents of its own. Distilled water is free of mineral impurities or chemical additives. You can purchase it in gallon jugs at a supermarket or drugstore.

You can make cologne from flowers or floral oils. Originally cologne was made by placing flowers in a jar filled with alcohol and a small amount of oil. As the jar set, the alcohol released the floral oils and the added oil absorbed them. Later the jar would be opened and the liquid poured into another container where it was mixed with water. This water was then used for baths. *Eau de cologne* is French for water of Cologne. Cologne is a city in Germany where cologne is said to have originated.

When making cologne, use an eye dropper to measure precious floral oils into unscented rubbing alcohol.

Use a funnel to pour the tincture or cologne into storage containers.

Glass stores cologne well as long as it has a tight seal. Consider using old cologne bottles.

Recipes

The following recipes are based on old French standards. You can substitute gums and resins for the old animal oils of musk, ambergris, and civet. You may use the animal oils, if you prefer, in place of the resins.

All measurements have been translated into familiar English standards, for your convenience.

ROSE PERFUME
1/16 ounce rose oil (attar of roses, if available)
1/16 ounce oil of rose geranium
1/4 ounce oil of bergamot
1 ounce tincture of benzoin
1/16 ounce tincture of orris root
14 ounces alcohol
2 ounces distilled water

ROSE COLOGNE
1 pint alcohol
2 quarts distilled water
2 ounces glycerin
1/4 ounce rose oil
1 ounce tincture of benzoin
1/4 ounce oil of rose geranium
1/4 ounce tincture of orris root

Roses have been used for their appearance, scent, and therapeutic properties throughout history. (Stark Bros. Nurseries & Orchards Co.)

BAY RUM AFTERSHAVE COLOGNE

½ ounce oil of bay leaves
2 ounces tincture of orange peel
10 ounces rum
1 teaspoon cinnamon
1 ounce tincture of benzoin
1 pint alcohol
3 quarts distilled water

BAY RUM AFTERSHAVE COLOGNE FROM BAY LEAVES

Stuff a quart jar with bay leaves. Fill it with alcohol, leaving 2 inches at the top of the jar. Add olive oil. Cover and let sit two or three days. Shake contents from time to time while the mixture is sitting.

Pour off the liquid into a gallon jug. To the liquid add:

1 ounce tincture of benzoin
1 ounce grated soap (optional, use a mild soap like Ivory)
10 ounces rum
1 pint alcohol
1 teaspoon cinnamon
3 quarts distilled water

This bay rum potpourri contains many of the same ingredients as would be used in cologne and aftershave recipes.

LAVENDER COLOGNE FROM FLOWERS
1 quart English lavender flowers packed tightly in jar

Fill jar with alcohol, leaving 2 inches at top. Add olive oil. Cover tightly and let sit two or three days, shaking the contents from time to time.

Pour off the liquid into a gallon jug. Add 1 ounce tincture of balsam Peru and 3 drops bergamot oil. Fill to top with distilled water.

LAVENDER COLOGNE
½ ounce lavender oil
3 drops oil of bergamot
1 ounce tincture of balsam Peru
1 pint alcohol
2 quarts distilled water

LILAC PERFUME
1/16 ounce lilac oil
1/16 ounce heliotrope oil
¼ ounce oil of bergamot
1 ounce tincture of benzoin
12 ounces alcohol
2 ounces distilled water

VIOLET PERFUME
1/16 ounce violet oil
1/16 ounce rose oil
1 ounce tincture of orris root
3 drops oil of bergamot
12 ounces alcohol
2 ounces distilled water

HELIOTROPE PERFUME
1/16 ounce heliotrope oil
1 ounce tincture of balsam Peru
3 drops oil of bergamot
12 ounces alcohol
2 ounces distilled water

NOSEGAY BOUQUET
¼ ounce rose oil
1/16 ounce violet oil
¼ ounce heliotrope oil
¼ ounce lilac oil
1 ounce tincture of balsam Tolu
12 ounces alcohol
2 ounces water (distilled)

TOILET WATERS

Toilet waters are similar to colognes, but they are not as potent. They are most often used in the same manner, after baths or after washing. They can be splashed on freely. They also can be used after shaving.

Toilet waters can be used to scent handkerchiefs and other personal articles, but they should not be so fragrant that their persistence is overwhelming. Like a whiff of a flower, they should leave a delicate impression.

LAVENDER WATER
10 ounces deodorized (unscented) alcohol
5 ounces water
1 drop oil of bergamot
½ ounce tincture of benzoin
3 drops lavender perfume or 2 drops oil of lavender

ORANGE BLOSSOM WATER
5 ounces water
10 ounces unscented alcohol
3 ounces tincture of orange blossom
1 drop oil of bergamot
1 drop orange oil

ROSE WATER
10 ounces unscented alcohol
5 ounces distilled water
3 drops rose perfume or 1 drop oil of rose
1 drop oil of rose geranium
½ ounce tincture of benzoin

AFTERSHAVES

The tangy, tingling sensation it causes after being splashed on is one way to describe an aftershave. Most aftershaves act as astringents; they help firm skin tone and close skin pores when applied immediately after shaving. Many aftershaves contain alcohol, which possesses antibacterial abilities, helping to prevent infections of knicks and shaving cuts. It also should contain glycerin and/or other ingredients known to be beneficial to skin care. Glycerin will help counter the drying effects of alcohol on the skin, and the chaffing and irritation that can develop with dry skin.

WITCH HAZEL AFTERSHAVE
2 ounces tincture of witch hazel
½ pint unscented alcohol
1 quart distilled water
1 ounce glycerin
1 ounce tincture of balsam Peru

SPICY AFTERSHAVE
1 teaspoon cinnamon
½ teaspoon cloves
1 ounce tincture of benzoin
1 ounce tincture of orange peel
1 drop oil of bergamot
½ pint alcohol
1 quart water

LEMON AFTERSHAVE
½ pint unscented alcohol
1 quart distilled water
1 ounce tincture of benzoin
1 drop bergamot oil
3 drops lemon oil or 2 ounces tincture of lemon peel
¼ teaspoon cinnamon

LIME AFTERSHAVE
1 drop oil of bergamot
2 drops lime oil
1 ounce tincture of benzoin
1 quart water
½ pint unscented alcohol

Chapter 10

Deodorants & Room Fresheners

DEODORANTS ARE EASY to make at home and can save money. All of the necessary ingredients are readily available at the store, and many ingredients you can make, yourself, at home.

LIQUID DEODORANT SPRAYS

To make liquid deodorant sprays, you should have the following equipment:

- ❀ A measuring cup
- ❀ A mixing container (glass jar with a tight lid)
- ❀ A pouring spout
- ❀ A nonaerosol spray bottle or atomizer

Atomizers work nicely, or you can use plant misters, which are available at most dime or hardware stores. They are economical and well suited to this purpose.

Liquid chlorophyll is available at most health food stores, or you can make your own from lawn clippings. If you are using lawn clippings, do not use any grass that has been treated with chemical herbicides. Herbicides can be extracted into the tincture along with the chlorophyll.

131

TINCTURE OF CHLOROPHYLL

Put grass clippings into a quart Mason jar. Pour 1 pint of alcohol into the jar. Add 2 tablespoons vegetable (liquid) oil. Seal the jar tightly. Wrap it with tape to prevent vapors from escaping.

Shake the jar well and let it sit for three days to a week. Shake the jar a few times each day to stir up the contents.

When the liquid is dark green, pour it off into another container. Seal the container after all the liquid is emptied into it. This is your tincture. Dispose of the solids in the other jar as you like.

UNSCENTED DEODORANT SPRAY
1 ounce tincture of benzoin
2 ounces glycerin
4 ounces alcohol
2 ounces distilled water
4 ounces tincture of chlorophyll

SPICE SPRAY DEODORANT
1 teaspoon cinnamon
1 teaspoon cloves
2 teaspoons nutmeg
1 ounce tincture of lemon peel
1 ounce glycerin
3 drops oil of bergamot
1 pint alcohol
3 ounces distilled water

Kitchen spices can be used to scent your deodorant.

ROSE SPRAY DEODORANT
1 ounce liquid chlorophyll
1 ounce tincture of balsam Tolu
8 ounces alcohol
2 ounces distilled water
3 drops rose perfume

WITCH HAZEL SPRAY DEODORANT
1 ounce glycerin
1 pint alcohol
1 ounce tincture of orange peel
4 ounces witch hazel cologne
1 ounce chlorophyll
1 ounce tincture of balsam Peru

HELIOTROPE SPRAY DEODORANT
1 ounce liquid chlorophyll
1 ounce tincture of benzoin
3 drops heliotrope perfume
1 drop oil of bergamot
1 pint alcohol
4 ounces distilled water

Note: Never spray deodorants into the face. Avoid contact with the eyes and avoid breathing in the vapors.

DEODORANT POWDERS

If you do not care for the sprays, powder deodorant is even easier to mix up.

UNDERARM DEODORANT POWDER
4 ounces talcum powder
2 ounces cornstarch
1 ounce baking soda
3 drops of your favorite scent (optional)

FOOT POWDER DEODORANT
2 ounces cornstarch
4 ounces unscented talcum powder
1 ounce baking soda
1 teaspoon powdered orris root
3 drops of your favorite scent (optional)

CREME DEODORANTS

If you prefer your deodorants in a creme base, try the following recipe.

ANTIPERSPIRANT DEODORANT CREME
8 ounces lanolin
2 ounces distilled water
1 ounce baking soda
2 ounces unscented talcum powder
1 ounce cornstarch
2 ounces alcohol
3 drops perfume (optional)

DEODORANT CREME
For those who are allergic to lanolin
4 ounces hydrogentated vegetable oil (such as Crisco)
2 ounces distilled water
2 ounces unscented talcum powder
1 ounce baking soda
1 ounce cornstarch
3 drops perfume (optional)

Whip the shortening as you would for a cake, then add the other ingredients a little at a time until all are blended in. Mix the perfume in at the end.

STICK DEODORANTS

You can make stick deodorants at home, although it requires a little more work than for making liquids, powders, or cremes. The secret is to use a wax base. Beeswax is ideal; paraffin also may be used.

To make stick deodorants, you need a large bowl, wooden spoon, and a pan to heat up the wax. You can use small juice glasses for molds, or the cardboard in toilet paper rolls.

3 ounces of unscented talcum powder
2 ounces of cornstarch
1 ounce baking soda
1 ounce liquid chlorophyll
2 ounces of alcohol
2 ounces of distilled water
8 ounces of beeswax or paraffin

Mix these ingredients in a bowl and stir thoroughly.

Heat wax in a pan over a pot of boiling water or on a very low burner. *Hot wax can be very dangerous, so handle with extreme caution.*

As the wax melts, remove from heat. Add the other ingredients and blend them in well. If the wax becomes too thick to be workable, heat again cautiously, and continue.

As the mixture starts to cool, but before it hardens, add the liquid chlorophyll and the fragrance.

Pour into molds. It is best to have your molds already prepared and waiting so that you do not run out of them while the wax is hardening. Let set.

When deodorant sticks have set, remove them from glass molds and store them in a large glass jar with a tight lid. A cookie jar will work nicely for this purpose. The deodorant sticks will have a longer life if they are stored in a closed container; otherwise they might shrivel. You can also store the sticks in individual plastic bags, such as plastic sandwich bags wrapped with a tie or ribbon.

For push-up deodorant sticks, use the empty cardboard rolls that come in toilet paper, decorated to disguise what they used to be, if you like. To push up deodorant, simply push up from the bottom slowly and the deodorant will rise. Store in plastic wrapping to prevent shrinkage that may result from evaporation.

Several things can go wrong. They are best avoided by careful attention to detail. First, the wax can get too hot or the mixture can catch fire. Heat the wax over hot water or use a low flame setting, and that likelihood will be diminished. *Never pour alcohol into hot wax.*

Second, the wax might not harden. To solve that problem, simply reheat the mixture and add more wax. (You will also need to add more liquid chlorophyll and fragrance after the wax has cooled.)

Third, the wax might get too hard. If the stick is too hard, it will not leave a thin film of wax and deodorant on you. To make it more pliable, reheat it. When it starts to cool, add more alcohol. Do not get carried away. If you add too much alcohol, you will need to add more wax.

Note: Everytime you need to reheat the deodorant, you will lose alcohol, which is antiseptic, and fragrance. Floral oils are very volatile and will rapidly evaporate when heated. You must, therefore, always add more chlorophyll and perfume to the mixture each time it cools, but before it hardens.

UNDERARM PADS

One of the solutions for underarm perspiration of yesteryear was the use of underarm pads to absorb the excess perspiration and odor. Since the invention of antiperspirants, the use of such pads has diminished greatly and very few stores sell them. However, they are an idea whose time is returning as more people become aware of the harsh and sometimes harmful chemicals that go into antiperspirants.

Underarm pads consist of a double layer of soft cotton. Some people add cotton batting in between the layers for extra thickness. You can pin them to an undershirt, or if you prefer you can sew straps on to them so they can be worn even without an undershirt.

For extra deodorizing qualities, you can apply baking soda to the pads before putting them on. The pads will absorb excess moisture, and the baking soda will help to eliminate unpleasant odors. People who perspire heavily will enjoy using these pads because they will help keep their outer garments free of perspiration and body odors.

To make underarm pads, simply cut out circles of soft cotton material; flannel works nicely. The circles should be large enough to cover your underarm area. It is better if they are too big than too small. If you like, you may add extra cotton batting between the two layers before you sew it together, or you may feel the material to see if you think it will be thick enough to suit your needs. You will need at least two layers of cloth.

It is important that you use an absorbent cotton cloth for these underarm pads. Never use nylon or any material that repels moisture.

If you plan to pin the pads to your shirts, then you are all set to use them. You might wish to make straps to eliminate the need for pins.

To make straps, simply cut straight pieces out of the same cotton material used to make the underarm pads. You do not need to use the same material since the purpose of the straps is merely to hold the pads in place. You might find it more comfortable, however, to use the soft cotton straps.

The best way to make a strap is to measure it on your own arms or on the arms of the person you are making the pads for. That way you can make a comfortable underarm pad that holds on without being too loose or too tight. If the pads are held too loosely, they might slip off, which will defeat their purpose. If held too tightly, they might irritate and be painful to wear. The pads should fit so that you can wear them during your usual daily routine without causing grief.

It is a good idea to make a number of pads at the same time. Although you can use the pads over and over, you might not want to wear the same pad too many times before washing it. If you make several pairs of pads, it will save you time between washings and keep you safe from embarrassing perspiration problems.

If you like, you can add a little perfume or cologne to your pads.

ROOM DEODORIZERS

Room deodorizers do more than add a pleasant scent to the room. The liquid sprays usually contain some alcohol, which has antiseptic qualities. (Alcohol can kill bacteria.) Chlorophyll is one of nature's own deodorants and helps to neutralize ugly household odors.

Be careful when using liquid sprays to not spray into the face or eyes. Also it is best to avoid inhaling vapors.

Room fresheners do not need to be liquid. Ordinary potpourri or sachets placed in a room will go a long way toward perfuming the air. A pot of coffee can be used as a room freshener. Almost everybody likes the scent of freshly brewed coffee.

You can scent room deodorants with whatever fragrances you like, and you can place different fragrances in the various rooms in your house. Lavender might be right for your bedroom, perhaps rose for the living room.

Cedar Chips

Some people like to use cedarwood chips for scenting a room. They are mostly used in closets and to protect linens and drawers from moths and other insects. They have a nice outdoor fragrance. For a real summertime fragrance, try the following recipe.

SUMMER ROOM FRESHENER
4 ounces cedarwood chips
2 ounces sandalwood chips
2 ounces balsam fir needles
2 ounces sweet woodruff
1 ounce orris root powder

Mix ingredients thoroughly, and place in an open dish. Set the dish somewhere that it will not be disturbed or accidentally bumped into.

Recipes For Room Fresheners

WITCH HAZEL ROOM DEODORANT
3 ounces tincture of witch hazel
1 ounce tincture of orange peel
1 teaspoon cinnamon
1 ounce tincture of benzoin
2 ounces liquid chlorophyll
4 ounces distilled water
16 ounces alcohol

LILAC BOUQUET ROOM DEODORANT
2 ounces liquid chlorophyll
1 drop oil of bergamot
3 drops lilac oil
1 ounce tincture of orris root
1 drop rose oil
1 drop jasmine oil
4 ounces distilled water
14 ounces alcohol

MEADOW BLEND ROOM FRESHENER
2 ounces tincture of sweet woodruff
1 ounce tincture of heather
1 ounce balsam Peru
2 ounces liquid chlorophyll
4 ounces distilled water
1 drop oil of lavender
1 drop oil of bergamot
16 ounces alcohol

BALSAM FIR ROOM DEODORANT

2 ounces liquid chlorophyll
3 ounces distilled water
16 ounces alcohol
1 ounce tincture of benzoin
2 ounces tincture of balsam fir

WINTERGREEN ROOM DEODORANT

2 ounces liquid chlorophyll
1 ounce balsam Peru
4 ounces distilled water
16 ounces alcohol
3 drops wintergreen oil

MINT ROOM FRESHENER

2 ounces liquid chlorophyll
1 ounce balsam Tolu
4 ounces distilled water
2 drops spearmint oil
2 drops peppermint oil
16 ounces alcohol

PINE ROOM FRESHENER

2 ounces tincture of pine needles
1 ounce tincture of balsam fir
1 ounce tincture of balsam Peru
4 ounces distilled water
2 ounces liquid chlorophyll
16 ounces alcohol

LEMON ROOM FRESHENER

2 ounces tincture of lemon peel
1 ounce tincture of lemongrass
1 ounce tincture of balsam Tolu
4 ounces distilled water
2 ounces liquid chlorophyll
16 ounces alcohol

ROSE ROOM FRESHENER

2 ounces liquid chlorophyll
1 ounce balsam Peru
½ ounce tincture of rose geranium
3 drops rose oil
2 ounces distilled water
12 ounces alcohol

Chapter 11
Shortcuts

UP TO THIS POINT, you have been instructed how to make a variety of toiletries and other products, using choice natural ingredients. This chapter presents suggestions on what to look for when you buy ready-made items, and short-cuts you can use to make or extend items for home use.

THINGS TO LOOK FOR WHEN YOU BUY

One of the easiest ways to check your buying is to stop buying some products altogether. Top on the list of what not to buy is any antiperspirant, no matter what the brand or how good an advertising campaign the company has. People sweat by nature. Sweat releases salts, toxic substances, and other body wastes. Repressing perspiration is not a good idea.

Once the antiperspirant effect wears off or is washed off, the person using that product begins "stinking like a skunk"—an absolutely horrible odor. A person becomes easily hooked on antiperspirants because of this extremely offensive odor, not realizing that he would not be experiencing anything that vile were it not for odors previously repressed.

If wetness disturbs you and you're wearing outer garments with sleeves, the solution is very simple. Wear a short-sleeved T-shirt underneath. They even have T-shirts with V-necks or low-cut curved fronts. You can also cut them as low as you choose, or wear underarm pads. If your garment is sleeveless, your perspiration will mostly evaporate while you work or play, especially when outdoors.

Most deodorants are far less harmful to your skin, your long-term general well-being, and sometimes, even to the atmosphere than anti-perspirants but it is a wise idea to read labels whenever you buy anything. Unlike deodorant salves, creams, powders, and certain sprays, deodorant soap is another product not worth buying. It is harsh on your skin—not any better in reducing grime than milder soaps—and the same chemicals that deodorize also reduce the body's natural protectants. When you buy soaps, don't be misled by brand names and advertising. Read the labels.

A mild soap like Ivory or one of the cold-cream soaps from Woolworths do well for most men or women. A really good Vitamin E soap from one of the health-food suppliers might be the best for anybody's skin, but even here, read the label. The use of mineral oil in products detracts from their value and benefit to your skin.

If you rarely do really grimy work (like tarring a roof, putting in an asphalt driveway, or painting with enamel), your best bet might be to merely use cooking oil on your spots. You can have someone else pour it over your hands, or you can do it yourself. Of course, if you regularly do "dirty work," it might pay you to keep one of the hand-scrubbing greasy cleaners on hand. Ordinarily, it should not be gritty. Oil—not grit—releases most grime. Again, read the label.

If you want to purchase perfume, test it for fragrance by loosening the cap slightly, then sniffing. Never open the bottle. Not only might they kick you out of the store, an open perfume bottle smells hideous. You get more alcohol than essence. And you can't usually smell it at all if the cover is on tight. The same is true of cologne or toilet water.

Shortcuts

A bowl of fruit on the table is not only a delight to the eyes, the right fruits or combinations produce an aromatic welcome to your guests—or to yourself as you enter after a hard day's work. Depsite their firm outer skin and rather hard interior, apples create a tantalizing perfume. You can merely walk into a room and immediately detect and appreciate the presence of apples. One or more apples in your fruit bowl is always good.

Oranges are a colorful addition to your selection. They have a pleasant aroma even unpeeled; however, you almost have to put them to your nose to detect it. A peeled orange has an entirely different effect. It causes a person entering a room to look around and sniff. Just before you expect special company, you might pare an orange. Leave the peeling encircling the fruit on a small bread-and-butter plate—as though you were just preparing to eat it. A small sharp knife on or beside the plate makes a good effect.

You can use any fruit you choose in your bowl. When using the real article, be sure they don't start rotting or shriveling. Bananas have a pleasing fragrance when ripe, but most people do not consider them very attractive at that stage. They have, in fact a "quick-sale" appearance and are extremely perishable.

It is possible to have a vegetable tray or to combine a few colorful vegetable items with your fruits. Winter squashes (although having no aroma) can add long-lasting and contrasting touches. If you use any vegetables that perish easily, like celery or even carrots, you might wish to use them as part of a meal or for snacks within a day or two (depending on the heat). Adding an apple or two to your display ensures a delicious fragrance, as well as adding red, yellow, or green tints.

Any perishable food, whether vegetable or fruit, should not be left out on the table indefinitely—and perhaps not at all in some climates or seasons. Cantalope, for example, has a delightful smell to entice a guest for the day. Your friend will rightfully expect to partake of that tasty morsel while visiting.

Wax fruits often look quite pretty, but they do require a little washing from time to time. One real red apple in their midst will provide the desired fragrance.

Of course, another way to create an irresistible aroma for a favored guest is through cooking. Make his favorite hot dish. Fresh-baked bread or muffins, still in the oven or fresh out of it, are a winner with almost anybody.

Sprinkling a tiny bit of spice on the cookstove just before company arrives is another temporary shortcut when you're out of those fabulous potpourris you're famous for. Cinnamon, allspice, or pumpkin-pie spice are your best choices. Obviously, you'll use the powdered or ground types for this purpose.

A few squirts of lemon juice in your tea adds an essence of lemon in the air. Even people who do not like coffee usually enjoy the smell of coffee brewing or steaming in the pot. Hot chocolate perfumes the air for some, while others are "turned-on" by mint—in a drink, over ice cream, or in a pan of hot water. A few drops of peppermint oil from the pharmacy will do, but a sprig or few leaves of peppermint, spearmint, or wintergreen from your own yard will be more visually and aesthetically pleasing.

Especially if you have children, you might find that bar soap dwindles to nothing and disappears in virtually no time. Or your family's washing habits might be such that small slivers of soap are either routinely tossed away or accumulate to the point where you feel like having a garage sale. You might have an added problem with children in that the high-quality soap you make or buy is always gritty after the children are through washing their hands. Some people solve this problem by confining their offspring to a specific bathroom or making them "hose off" outside before entering the house. That just means that the soap doesn't get *quite* as sandpapery a texture. (Kids are rather innovative. If your house is spotless, your child will merely drop the soap onto his overturned shoe, for example.)

A more sensible shortcut is to take all those little pieces of soap and put them into a spray-pump container which previously held hand lotion, shampoo, or liquid soap. Add hot water and shake well. If you choose, you can add a capful or teaspoon of other ingredients, such as shampoo, bubble bath, olive oil, etc. Although it might be "soup" a little faster, it really isn't necessary to add anything but the soap and water. Everytime you get a new sliver, you can add it into the jar, along with more hot water if necessary. It's also handy for adults who routinely do dirty tasks, such as fixing wood fires or messing around with the lawn mower.

If your kids are "driving you nuts" some summer day (and you have a safe place for them to blow bubbles, the liquid soap used in your kitchen for dishes works well as a replacement for the little bottles of colored concoction they likely spill or otherwise waste the first day they play with it. Let them use it full strength, or dilute it with water.

If you like a floral-scented (pine-scented, or other perfumed) sachet nestling among your nightwear, lingerie, underwear, or clothes drawer, you will certainly want to make one or appreciate getting one from a friend. You might have lost all of yours in a recent move, however, and lack the time to make more. What do you do? The easiest answer is to place a bar of soap with your favorite essence in each of the drawers or other places where you would like to impart a little fragrance. Some of the tiny bars motels give their guests work very well. Unwrap the soap or not, as you choose. Whenever you think of it—perhaps while rummaging for a special pair of socks or other item—merely move the bar from one position to another to spread the aromatic effect.

A bamboo basket is an excellent container for soaps stored among linens.

142

Don't expect to impress your friends by giving them a Holiday Inn or Howard Johnson's bar and saying, "Here's a sachet for you." This is just an "emergency" shortcut for yourself. Your friends and customers will want those lovely sachets containing your own roses or lilacs and all the other natural ingredients you will carefully select.

For a quick sachet, empty potpourri into a plastic lunch bag.

143

If you realize you're out of deodorant and have important plans some Sunday, don't panic. Merely run into the kitchen and shake a little baking soda into your hand. Put some into your other hand. Rub your underarm areas. If you have a foot problem, sprinkle some into your socks or shoes. If you want your "private" area protected, do not rub it on. Just shake a little from your fingertips into your underwear.

After reading this chapter, you might come up with emergency shortcuts of your own. Remember, *none* will touch the high quality of your own natural garden creations.

Untie the bag when you want a whiff of fragrance.

Chapter 12

Selling Your Creations

WHEN MAKING POTPOURRIS for sale, it is important to remember that the customer's needs must be met. Some items are more popular than others. Lemon, for example is a popular scent. It might be worth your while to stock faster selling items for volume sales. Other people have unique tastes and might favor unusual scents, like tangerine, grapefruit, or bergamot.

Whatever you are selling, do not be afraid to make those items that especially appeal to you. You will also want to make the popular items, however, if you want to make any money.

MAKING THE PACKAGE FIT THE MARKET

Appearances are all important in marketing. People do "judge a book by its cover." They also judge everything else by the way that it is packaged. People are more willing to pay a premium for fancy packages.

You want to capitalize on the public thirst for homemade products. Your creations must look just as good as store-bought ones, but the packages generally should not be quite as sleek. A too-fancy package might look commercial and hurt sales. People will forgive a few imperfections if they think they are buying a quality homemade product, but use reason. People expect certain standards of quality and fairness in any product. Soap bars, for instance, should be fairly exact in size and measure. If they are off by too much, the customer will be repelled. People want to get their money's worth, and more! Soap cakes cannot be one size one week, and smaller the next.

FINDING MARKETS

There is a market for just about everything under the sun. That market does not operate in a void, however. There is always competition for the consumer's dollar. You will have to decide which market is the right one for you. Usually the safest bet is to specialize in one or two items and carve out a niche in the marketplace for your product. The safe path is also a well-worn one, however, and you might want to diversify. The idea behind diversity is that you are not "putting all your eggs in one basket."

Whatever you decide, it is usually best to start on a small scale and let your business grow as the market demands. Most big firms follow this principle. They always test-market any new product before releasing it to the general public.

(Thistledown)

Types of Markets

There are many types of markets. Most involve direct sales and personal contact. In mail-order sales, you lack face-to-face contact, but the sales are still direct (ordinarily).

When you sell to a retailer who then sells to individual customers, you are involved in *indirect sales*. You might find a store or outlet near you interested in buying and reselling your wares. If you produce the volume necessary, it is conceivable you could even sell to a chain of stores.

Roadside Stands

If you live in the country, you might want to set up a roadside stand during the warm months. This is quite advantageous if you also sell fruits and vegetables. For your stand to succeed, you should be located within 50 miles of a medium to large city, on a well-traveled highway.

Have adequate parking spaces and signs to point out your stand. If you live in a city, you will have to check out the zoning regulations of selling in your home.

Flea Markets

Flea markets bring out all kinds of people, but they all have one thing in common: most are looking for bargains. Because of this, it is probably ill-advised to try to sell high-priced items. Your best bet is to sell a low-priced item in volume.

Farmer's Markets

There are many cities that now have farmer's markets. At these, for a small fee, people can sell homegrown or homemade products. You will usually do quite well at these sites if you develop a steady clientele of customers. Items can be priced higher than at flea markets, but usually lower than in retail shops.

148

Chain Stores

If you can get your items into one of the chain stores, you should do well. Chain stores sell in volume, but they also expect certain standards and delivery according to strict time schedules. To sell to a chain, you might want to make a sample of the item complete with packaging for demonstration. Remember, they are in business to make a profit, so sales are likely to be on a *consignment* basis, which means that the company agrees to sell the product, returning to you the ones it does not sell. You receive your money only as the product sells.

Commission Sales

Consignment sales will be the likely route of most retail stores. You might however, be able to talk smaller shops into commission sales. With commission sales, you must provide the store with a commission, premium, or other incentive to promote the sale of your product over others.

HOW TO PRICE

Before you price any item, you must take many factors into consideration. First, you must include the total cost of producing the item, including packaging and time spent for labor. Then it is always wise to leave some room for price changes of the basic ingredients (costs to you).

149

A good rule of thumb is to add 20 percent of the cost of an item as a profit margin for you. Anything higher might affect costs to your customers and lower sales. Lower profits will allow you to sell cheaper, but do not leave you much of a safety margin for unexpected costs.

Pricing also depends upon where you are selling your product—flea market versus retail store—as well as how you package the product. Better prices come with fancy wrappings.

After you have determined your cost (including your time and labor), you should check the prices of your competition. Do not worry about the commercial producers as much as those who are also offering homemade products. Naturally, you can charge more for a cake of homemade soap than a commercial one, but your charges should not be too far out of line. If you charge too much, people might decide to shop where they can get it cheaper. If you do not charge enough, people might think your product is inferior or you would not sell it so cheap. If including your time and labor tends to put your prices out of line with your competition, you can adjust your figure as you choose; after all, you're the boss.

Multicolored candles are always popular. (Country Treasures)

INSURANCE

Most small-scale operators do not need to worry about insurance. If you start marketing on a large scale, however, you will want some type of business insurance to protect you from lawsuits.

SECRETS OF SUCCESS

Many books have been written on how to succeed in business. America's companies spend millions on research, and students train in business schools for years. They all want to know the "secrets" of success in the business world. You can spend a fortune learning how to be successful, or you can accept the common sense fact that for anyone to be successful in business, you need customers. It is customers, or lack of them, that make or break businesses. One goal of advertising is to increase the number of customers; another is to keep their loyalty.

Sell with Sizzle

Another secret of sales is to sell with sizzle! Whenever you deal with the public on a direct basis, you are also selling yourself. Your attitude and enthusiasm (or lack of it) will reflect on the product. If you had a rough night, the chances are you will sell less than if you came in feeling exuberant. Remember, happiness and enthusiasm are contagious. Don't be afraid to be friendly. People appreciate it. The world is filled with frightened and lonely people. The smile you give them might be the only one they get all week. Make it a genuine smile. If the customers like you, they are more likely to like your wares.

Complaints

One of the problems in dealing with the public is that there seem to be some people who can never be satisfied. They are chronic complainers. Most people will present legitimate complaints. The best way to handle complaints is to assume the customer is always right—whether they are or not. After all, you need them a lot more than they need you. So try to appease customers as best you can. Whatever you do, don't let the complainers spoil your sunny disposition, or it will cost you in sales.

Another secret of business is the fact that real money is made from repeat business. One sale is fine and dandy, but you want to keep 'em coming back for more! As long as you can get that repeat business, you will succeed.

Economic growth is an organic process. That is, it starts small and grows bigger.

Other Considerations

Consider your own perspective. It is best to sell only a product that you honestly like. Do not try to make something because you think it will make you rich. Most "get-rich-quick" schemes do not pan out. Be honest with yourself, and your honesty will show through to your customers. If you earn the respect of your customers, you also will likely receive their loyalty.

Do not limit yourself, nor let your friends try to limit you—no matter how well their intentions. If you allow other people to determine your identity, in effect to tell you who you are and how to behave, then you are not in control of your own life. You need to have more than ambition to succeed in business; you need to have patience and the ability to control what's going on as best you can.

If you allow other people to tell you what you can and cannot do, you will be surrendering even before you begin. Remember that a positive, cheerful attitude helps sell. You will sell your best when you are happy and having fun. When your eyes sparkle and your voice chimes, people are going to want to buy from you.

Let the Product Sell Itself

For the most part avoid the "hard sell." If somebody does not want to buy your product, it is a waste of your time and energy trying to force them into buying it. Although you can intimidate some customers by this method, most people will be turned off. Potential customers might even be lost, because few people like salespeople who are too pushy. If you are asked about the product, list a few good points, then let the customer make up his mind.

Don't just sell goods—sell goodwill. Make your customers want to come back again and again. (Thistledown)

In a Nutshell

Here are a few simple good business practices.

1) Smile. Smiling faces are always more attractive than expressionless ones, or worse yet, those with a frown. The smile you give might be the only one your customer gets all day. Make it a genuine one.

2) Be friendly. Friendliness is always appreciated. People might forget what they bought, but they always remember how they were treated.

3) Have a positive attitude. Happiness and enthusiasm are contagious.

4) Never argue. It is all right to disagree, but be civil when doing it.

5) Be honest. People are not as naive as they might appear. They appreciate honesty, and it creates a feeling of trust, which is good for business.

6) Go for repeat sales. You want the customer to come back and bring friends. Give the customer his money's worth and a little more. Samples, premiums, and other freebies are bound to bring in more business then they cost, and are well worth using.

There are other tricks of the trade. Most of them you will learn as you do business.

Appendix
Mail-Order Supplies

MOST OF THE ITEMS that will you need for making potpourris, sachets, and soaps will be available at local stores. Some items, however, such as fixing agents for helping the fragrance last in our scented products, are rarer. You might need to go to a specialty shop to obtain them, or you can order them from a mail-order supply house.

Mail-order companies are very convenient and are frequently able to supply you with items that other sources cannot. An order usually takes only a few weeks or less to arrive. If, like some people, you are very impatient and do not like to wait, be sure to make a checklist before ordering. List every item that you will need to complete a project. You might even want to make more than one checklist if you plan on doing other projects. It is very efficient and usually quite economical to order by mail.

There is less likelihood of whimsical purchases because you have a chance to add up the costs and know exactly how much you are spending before you ever send the order. Often, when shopping at stores other items catch your eye, and you spend much more money than you intended. When ordering by mail, you have the advantage of sitting down and thinking about what you need and how much money you want to spend. If you want to stay within your budget, you can choose items then selectively cross some off your list. This is much more difficult to do when shopping in a store.

Following is a list of mail-order firms that sell the items you might find useful in preparing your homemade scented products. This list is not all-exhaustive, but rather provides you with several reputable dealers. Information as to what the company specializes in and cost, if any, of its catalog or price list is included. Companies might offer additional items not listed. Be sure to check the individual catalogs.

MAIL-ORDER SUPPLIERS

EDMUND SCIENTIFIC
101 E. Gloucester Pike, Barrington, NJ 08007
Kits for perfume-making; glass bottles, and containers

GENERAL NUTRITION
418 Wood, Pittsburgh, PA 15222
Herbal powders; liquid chlorophyll

HERRSCHNER'S
Stevens Point, WI 54481
Candle yarn; linen; cloth; embroidery equipment

INDIANA BOTANIC GARDENS
P. O. Box 5, Hammond, IN 46325
Catalog: $0.25
Floral oils; herbs; resins; beeswax; apothecary jars and perfume bottles

OLDS SEED CO.
P. O. Box 7790, Madison, WI 53707
Kits for drying flowers; silica gel; flower seeds; fruit plants

ORIGINAL SWISS AROMATICS
P. O. Box 606, San Rafael, CA 94915
Essential oils; aromatherapy supplies; books; glass bottles

PENN HERB
603 North Second, Philadelphia, PA 19123
Catalog: $1.00
Herbs; oils

THE SOAP OPERA
319 State St. Madison, WI 53703
Soaps; essential oils; perfume-making supplies; potpourris

WHITE FLOWER FARM
Litchfield, CT 06759
Catalog: $5.00
Flower seeds

MAIL–ORDER FRUITS

The following are mail-order nursery houses that specialize in fruits.

BOUNTIFUL RIDGE NURSERIES, INC.
P. O. Box 250, Princess Anne, MD 21853

CALIFORNIA NURSERY CO.
P. O. Box 2278, Fremont, CA 94536

DEAN FOSTER NURSERIES
Hartford, MI 49057

FARMER SEED AND NURSERY CO.
818 NW 4th, Faribault, MN 55021

GURNEY SEED AND NURSERY
Yankton, SD 57078

STARK BRO'S NURSERIES
Louisiana, MO 63353

MAIL–ORDER PLANTS

The following are mail-order nursery houses that specialize in flower and or herb plants and seeds.

BLUESTONE PERENNIALS
7247 Middle Ridge Rd., Madison, OH 44057
Perennials, ready for transplanting

CAPRILANDS
Coventry, Connecticut 06238
Herbs, Potpourris, etc.

HALCYON GARDEN HERBS
P. O. Box 124 CR, Gibsonia, PA 15044
$1.00 for catalog guide to growing herbs

MELLINGERS NURSERY, INC.
2310 W. South Range Rd., North Lima, OH 44452
Seeds and young plants

ROSES OF YESTERDAY AND TODAY
802 Brown's Valley Rd., Watsonville, CA 95076
Roses

Appendix

R. H. SHUMWAY SEEDSMAN
628 Cedar, Rockford, IL 61101
Flower seeds

WAYSIDE GARDENS
Hodges, SC 29695
Catalog: $1.00
Young transplants, wildflowers, and perennials

Index